Remember, O Yahweh

Remember, O Yahweh

The Poetry and Context of Psalms 135–137

JAMES M. TODD III

WIPF & STOCK · Eugene, Oregon

REMEMBER, O YAHWEH
The Poetry and Context of Psalms 135–137

Copyright © 2015 James M. Todd III. All rights reserved. Except for brief quotations in critical publications or reviews, no part of this book may be reproduced in any manner without prior written permission from the publisher. Write: Permissions, Wipf and Stock Publishers, 199 W. 8th Ave., Suite 3, Eugene, OR 97401.

Wipf & Stock
An Imprint of Wipf and Stock Publishers
199 W. 8th Ave., Suite 3
Eugene, OR 97401

www.wipfandstock.com

ISBN 13: 978-1-4982-1882-5

Manufactured in the U.S.A.   08/28/2015

To Christina, my beautiful and virtuous wife

Contents

List of Tables | viii
Preface | ix
Acknowledgments | xi
List of Abbreviations | xiii

Introduction | 1

Part 1: The Poetry of Psalms 135–137
1 Poetic Analysis of Psalm 135 | 9
2 Poetic Analysis of Psalm 136 | 37
3 Poetic Analysis of Psalm 137 | 59

Part 2: The Context of Psalms 135–137
4 Contextual Analysis of the Psalm Group 135–137 | 85
5 Psalms 135–137 in the Context of Book V | 99

Conclusion | 127

Bibliography | 131

Tables

Table 1. Structural Parallels between Psalms 135 and 136 | 86
Table 2. Thematic Parallels between Psalms 135 and 136 | 86
Table 3. Lexical Parallels between Psalms 135 and 136 | 87
Table 4. Thematic Parallels between Psalms 135–136 and 137 | 94
Table 5. Lexical Parallels between Psalms 135–136 and 137 | 94
Table 6. Lexical Parallels between Psalms 134 and 135 | 100
Table 7. Lexical Parallels between Psalms 133 and 135 | 102
Table 8. Lexical Parallels between Psalms 135–137 and 138 | 112

Preface

This book is a revision of my 2010 doctoral dissertation entitled "A Poetic and Contextual Analysis of Psalms 135–137." My revisions are the most extensive in the "Introduction" and first part of the book (the poetic analyses of the individual psalms). I only made a few minor changes in the second half of the book (contextual analysis), wherein I incorporated a few additional works, one being a doctoral dissertation that interacted with my dissertation.

Several changes that I made in my poetic analyses merit discussion. Perhaps the most significant change involved my observations of phonological parallels. In my original dissertation, I went rogue too often with phonological parallels. In this work, I have submitted myself to Berlin's phonological controls (see "Introduction"). Moreover, I relegate many of my discussions of phonological parallels to the footnotes. Most of the phonological parallels serve a supporting role to the semantic and lexical parallels present in the psalms, thus limiting their interpretive significance.

The second major change in the first part of the book relates to the morphological parallels between poetic lines. Since almost all of the morphological parallels I noted in my dissertation had minimal interpretive significance, I have chosen not to discuss them in this book. They are undoubtedly important for enhancing the parallelism of adjacent lines, but I removed them due to space limitations.

I hope this book continues the ongoing dialogue of the meaning of the Psalter. In particular, Book V is important in bringing to a close the many textual tapestries of the Psalter, and if my analysis of this psalm group can help move the discussion one step further, then my labor has not been in vain.

Acknowledgments

This book marks the culmination of a long process during which the Lord has been abundantly faithful and good to me. Any glory or accolades that might come because of this work belong to him alone. My ultimate hope is that this book leads people to do as Ps 136:1 commands: "Give thanks to the Lord for he is good, for his loving-kindness endures forever."

The person whose fingerprints are everywhere in this book is Dr. Robert Cole. He gave me valuable insights during the writing of my dissertation and continued to be a source of encouragement throughout the revision and publication of this book. Dr. Cole's sensitivity to the nuances of Hebrew poetry and the canonical shaping of the Psalter provide a model for me and all serious students of the Psalter.

When it comes to my dissertation, two other professors were of great assistance. My second reader was Dr. Mark Rooker. I am thankful for Dr. Rooker's willingness to serve in this capacity and for his valuable feedback. Also, Dr. David Howard generously served as my outside reader. To have such a pioneer in Psalter studies read and offer feedback on my dissertation was a significant blessing. He was the first person to challenge me to publish my work, and he has continued to give me encouragement and advice as I have kept him updated on its publication status.

The person who has had the greatest impact upon my scholarship is Dr. John Sailhamer. His deep love for Scripture and his passion for teaching is what first drew me into Old Testament studies. I am thankful for the few years I had to sit under his tutelage at Southeastern Baptist Theological Seminary.

Three other men sacrificially gave their time and energy to assist me in the dissertation. The benefits of their work on the dissertation are evident in this revision. Aime Kidimbu translated several important French articles for me, while Wesley Handy and Andy Witt both read portions of my dissertation and provided solid feedback and encouragement. Without their careful reading, this book would have many more deficiencies.

I also want to thank Wipf and Stock Publishers for publishing this work. In particular, a special thanks to Matthew Wimer, who patiently endured many questions from this rookie author and did a great job of communicating at every stage of the publication process.

Finally, there is my family. My parents have consistently supported and encouraged me over the years. Their support has been invaluable. Last, but certainly not least . . . my biggest fans are my wife and my children. Throughout the process of writing the dissertation, the free and joyful spirits of my children renewed my energy. Now, five years later, their joy and exuberance for life continue to remind me of what is most important. Last, the MVP of my dissertation and this revision is my wife Christina. Her constant support, love, and encouragement have carried me through thick and thin. The small sacrifices I have made pale in comparison with the enormous sacrifices she has made for me over the years.

Abbreviations

ATANT	Abhandlungen zur Theologie des Alten und Neuen Testaments
BBB	Bonner biblische Beiträge
BDB	Brown, Francis, S. R. Driver, and Charles A. Briggs. *A Hebrew and English Lexicon of the Old Testament*
Bib	*Biblica*
BibInt	*Biblical Interpretation*
BK	*Bibel und Kirche*
BSac	*Bibliotheca Sacra*
CBQ	*Catholic Biblical Quarterly*
BK	*Bibel unk Kirche*
BZ	*Biblische Zeitschrift*
FOTL	Forms of the Old Testament Literature
HALOT	*The Hebrew and Aramaic Lexicon of the Old Testament*. Ludwig Koehler, Walter Baumgartner, and Johann J. Stamm. Translated and edited under the supervison of Mervyn E. J. Richardson. 4 vols. Leiden: Brill, 1994–1999
HAR	*Hebrew Annual Review*
HBT	*Horizons in Biblical Theology*
ICC	International Critical Commentary
Int	*Interpretation*
JBL	*Journal of Biblical Literature*
JETS	*Journal of the Evangelical Theological Society*
JSOT	*Journal for the Study of the Old Testament*
JSOTSup	Journal for the Study of the Old Testament Supplement Series

Abbreviations

LHBOTS	Library of Hebrew Bible/Old Testament Studies
NCB	New Century Bible
NIB	*The New Interpreter's Bible*. Edited by Leander E. Keck. 12 vols. Nashville: Abingdon, 1994–2004
ÖBS	Österreichische biblische Studien
OTL	Old Testament Library
OTS	Old Testament Studies
SBB	Stuttgarter biblische Beiträge
SBLDS	Society of Biblical Literature Dissertation Series
SBLMS	Society of Biblical Literature Monograph Series
ScEs	*Science et esprit*
TBC	Torch Bible Commentaries
VT	*Vetus Testamentum*
VTSup	Supplements to Vetus Testamentum
WBC	Word Biblical Commentary
WTJ	*Westminster Theological Journal*
ZAW	Zeitschrift für die alttestamentliche Wissenschaft

Introduction

One of the distinguishing characteristics of Psalms' research in recent decades has been a focus on the final form of the MT Psalter. Following Brevard Childs, Gerald Wilson's groundbreaking dissertation demonstrated that purposeful editorial activity was evident in the final MT Psalter and thus introduced a new phase in Psalms studies.[1] Although form criticism continues to exert influence in the field, canonical analysis has solidified a dominant presence.

Over the past three decades, numerous studies devoting significant attention to the literary context of individual psalms have appeared. With regard to Book V of the Psalter, several authors have analyzed the entire book,[2] while others have studied the various groups of psalms within the book.[3] If we exclude Pss 146–150 (the conclusion to the entire Psalter), then every psalm group in Book V has been the object of a detailed study except four psalms: 119, 135, 136, and 137. These final three psalms are the object of the present investigation.

In this work, I treat Pss 135–137 as a group not because they share a common superscription[4] but because two major sub-collections—the Songs of Ascents (Pss 120–134) and the Last Davidic Psalter (Pss 138–145)—bracket them. The lack of a detailed contextual analysis of these three psalms leaves a vacuum in studies related to Book V, so this study

---

1. Wilson, *Editing*.

2. Goulder, *Psalms of the Return*. Leuenberger (*Konzeptionen*) and Ballhorn (*Zum Telos*) both examined Books IV and V.

3. Davis, "Contextual Analysis"; Keet, *Psalms of Ascents*; Seybold, *Die Wallfahrtpsalmen*; Crow, *Songs of Ascents*; Buysch, *Der letzte Davidpsalter*.

4. None of these psalms has a superscription. Psalm 135 is classified as a hallelujah psalm and Ps 136 as a hodu-psalm.

seeks to meet this deficiency and interact with various proposals regarding the function of these three psalms in Book V.

This book applies a comprehensive poetic and contextual analysis to Pss 135–137 in order to explain the meaning of each psalm, to determine the relationship of each psalm to the other psalms within this group, and to evaluate the group's possible function within Book V (Pss 107–150) of the Psalter. My thesis is that Pss 135–137, by means of the remembrance motif, serve as a bridge between the two major psalm groups in the second half of Book V (The Songs of Ascents and the Last Davidic Psalter). As such, Yahweh's past deliverance of Israel from their enemies (Pss 135–136) serves as the basis for Israel's prayer for future deliverance from their enemies (Ps 137). In turn, the psalm groups bordering Pss 135–137 connect Yahweh's ultimate restoration of Israel (and hence their future deliverance from their enemies) to Yahweh's remembrance of a future Davidic king (Ps 132) who will suffer at the hand of his enemies and be delivered (Ps 144).

RESEARCH METHODOLOGY

My methodology corresponds to the two primary aims of this book. First, I analyze the poetry of these psalms in order to interpret each psalm in the psalm group 135–137.[5] Second, I explore the psalms' canonical context through a contextual analysis of each psalm and the group as a whole. There is an inherent connection between these two aspects (poetic and contextual) as the poetic analysis of each psalm sets the stage for the contextual analysis that follows. Robert Cole rightly notes, "Often rhetorical analysis of individual poems contributes to understanding their role in the continuing dialogue . . ." of the Psalter.[6] Therefore, the present work begins at the lowest level of the psalm and works up to the highest level of the Psalter.

---

5. Throughout this book, I use the following poetic terms and definitions from Watson, *Classical*, 11–15: 1) Colon: A single line of poetry, either as a semi-independent unit (mono-colon), or as a part of a larger strophe (bi-colon, tri-colon, quatrain, etc.); 2) Bi-colon: A couplet made up of two cola; 3) Tri-colon: A set of three cola forming a single whole; 4) Strophe: A strophe is a verse-unit of one or more cola considered as part of the higher unit termed the stanza; and 5) Stanza: A sub-section of a poem: the poem is made up of stanzas, and each stanza consists of one or more strophes.

6. Cole, *Shape and Message*, 10. In my rhetorical analysis of Ps 136, I discovered that vv. 23–24 are rhetorically distinct from the rest of the psalm. Interestingly, the majority of connections between Pss 136 and 137 involve these two verses (see chapter 4).

INTRODUCTION

In this work, I do not blaze new methodological trails for the study of the Psalter; rather, I simply apply established methodologies to a specific group of psalms. Specifically, I incorporate three approaches: 1) the study of parallelism in Hebrew poetry, 2) rhetorical criticism, and 3) contextual criticism. The first two methods play a significant role in the poetic analysis of the individual psalms, and the final method is, as its name implies, limited to the study of the relationships between individual psalms and their surrounding psalms.

My approach to paralellism in Hebrew poetry depends primarily upon Adele Berlin's important work on this topic. Following Berlin, I examine parallelism in every linguistic area (i.e., phonological, grammatical, lexical, and semantic)[7] and "take a global view" of parallelism by not restricting parallelism to "adjacent lines or sentences," but extending it to the level of the psalm.[8] Moreover, I use her categories of syntagmatic and paradigmatic parallelism on the lexical and semantic levels,[9] and I employ her phonological "controls" in my analysis of the phonological parallels.[10] Finally, I often supplement her categories with those of Wilfred Watson[11] and Robert Alter.[12]

The second aspect of my poetic analysis of the individual psalms is rhetorical analysis. My rhetorical analysis builds upon a long line of interpreters that goes back to James Muilenburg's 1968 SBL Presidential Address, "Form Criticism and Beyond"[13] and involves three areas of investigation: 1) the structure of each psalm, 2) markers of turning points,[14]

---

7. Berlin, *Dynamics*, 28. Although Berlin refers to "linguistic aspects," I have used "linguistic levels" to refer to the different linguistic categories.

8. Ibid., 3.

9. Ibid., 72.

10. Ibid., 105. She lists the following controls for phonological parallelism: 1) it must involve "at least two sets of consonants," 2) "the sets must be in close proximity," and 3) the consonants must be "same or similar consonants" ("identical phoneme, an allophone . . . , or two phonemes which are articulated similarly").

11. Watson, *Classical*, 114–159.

12. Alter, *Art*.

13. James Muilenburg, "Form Criticism and Beyond." In outlining his primary objective, Muilenburg (8) states, "What I am interested in, above all, is in understanding the nature of Hebrew *literary composition*, in exhibiting the structural patterns that are employed for the fashioning of a literary unit, whether in poetry or in prose, and in discerning the many and various devises by which predications are formulated and ordered into a unified whole."

14. Lugt (*Cantos and Strophes*, 77–80) has done significant work in this area.

and 3) stylistic devices.[15] My study of the rhetorical features not only helps determine the psalm's meaning but also lays a foundation for the contextual analysis that follows.

A contextual analysis of Pss 135–137 completes the present investigation of these psalms. My contextual analysis agrees with many other microstructural studies of the Psalter's canonical shape.[16] On a broad level, it has the most in common with Cole's dissertation on Book III, in which he undergirds his canonical analysis with a detailed rhetorical analysis of each psalm.[17] More specifically, my approach shares many similarities with those of David Howard[18] and Gianni Barbiero.[19]

Throughout my contextual analysis, I highlight lexical, thematic, and structural connections between these psalms and their neighbors. Regarding lexical parallels, I only discuss the most significant parallels[20] based on three criteria:[21] 1) the lexeme's relationship to the major themes of the psalms, 2) the frequency of the lexeme (in the section of the Psalter, the Psalter as a whole, and/or the Hebrew Bible as a whole),[22] and 3) the location of the lexeme in the psalm.[23]

---

15. In her explication of Muilenburg's method, Trible (*Rhetorical Criticism*, 28) writes, "Attention to both features [structure and style] discloses the art of Hebrew composition."

16. I have borrowed the term "microstructural" from Howard, "Psalms and Current Study," 24. Howard identifies approaches that deal with "overarching patterns and themes" as macrostructural and those that deal with "connections among smaller groupings of psalms, especially adjacent psalms" as microstructural.

17. Cole, "Rhetorics and Canonical Structure."

18. Howard, *Structure*.

19. Barbiero, *Das erste Psalmenbuch*.

20. I have chosen not to distinguish between keyword links and thematic word links as Howard (*Structure*, 100–101) does. In this regard, my approach is similar to Barbiero's approach. Howard defines "key-word links" as "important words that were undoubtedly present in the editors' thinking" (p. 100). Such a criterion makes verification extremely difficult. In my own analysis, I find the distinction between Howard's "key-word links" and "thematic word links" too subjective.

21. Howard cites the first two of these factors. See Howard, *Structure*, 100–101; idem, "Contextual Reading," 117.

22. Howard ("Contextual," 117) argues that the juxtaposition of a rare term in two psalms "favors its identification as a key word." Cole (*Shape and Message*, 236–39) highlights the interpretive significance of *dis legomena* in identifying the "editorial hand(s)" in a psalm group (p. 239).

23. This criterion is dependent upon the rhetorical analysis of the individual psalms. If the lexeme is located in a compositionally significant verse, it may carry more weight.

INTRODUCTION

OVERVIEW OF THE BOOK

This book consists of two major parts. The first section (chapters 1–3) consists of the poetic analysis of the three psalms under consideration. The layout of each of these three chapters is uniform. After an outline of the psalm, the remainder of each chapter is the poetic analysis proper. The poetic analysis contains a verse-by-verse discussion of the content of each psalm grouped according to its stanzas and strophes (demarcated in that psalm's outline). The explanations of the individual verses proceed in accordance with the specific textual features of each verse and take into consideration the psalms's parallelism and rhetorical features.

The second section (chapters 4 and 5) is devoted to the contextual analysis of Pss 135–137. In chapter 4, I discuss the lexical, thematic, and structural parallels between Pss 135–137. Chapter 5 builds on the findings of chapter 4 and extends the investigation of parallels to the two psalm groups on either side of Pss 135–137. The last section of chapter 5 offers insights on the function of Pss 135–137 in the overall structure of Book V of the Psalter.

For an example see Cole, *Shape and Message*, 10.

Part 1

The Poetry of Psalms 135–137

1

Poetic Analysis of Psalm 135

OUTLINE

I. Introductory Call to Praise Yahweh (vv. 1–4)
    A. Yahweh's Servants Are Summoned to Praise (vv. 1–2)
    B. Reasons for the Praise of Yahweh (vv. 3–4)

II. Yahweh's Superiority over All Gods (vv. 5–18)
    A. Yahweh's Superior Greatness (vv. 5–6)
        1. Thematic Verse: Yahweh's Superior Greatness (v. 5)
        2. Primary Proof of Yahweh's Superior Greatness: Freedom to Act as He Pleases (v. 6)
    B. Specific Examples of Yahweh's Superior Greatness (vv. 7–12)
        1. Yahweh's Crafting of Storms (v. 7)
        2. Yahweh's Historical Victories (vv. 8–12)
            a. Yahweh's Defeat of Egypt (vv. 8–9)
            b. Yahweh's Defeat of the Kingdoms on the East and West of the Jordan (vv. 10–12)
    C. Confession of Yahweh's Eternal Renown (vv. 13–14)
        1. Praise for Yahweh's Eternal Renown (v. 13)
        2. Reason for Yahweh's Eternal Renown: His Care for His People (v. 14)
    D. Polemic Against Idols and Their Worshipers (vv. 15–18)

III. Concluding Call to Bless Yahweh (vv. 19–21)

A. A Call to Bless Yahweh (vv. 19–20)

B. Yahweh is Blessed from Zion (v. 21)

POETIC ANALYSIS

One of the distinguishing features of Ps 135 is its numerous allusions to other psalms and OT texts. In fact, almost every verse within this psalm corresponds to another biblical text.[1] Hans-Peter Mathys comments concerning this feature of the psalm: "If the term 'mosaic' applies to a psalm, then it applies to Ps 135."[2] Nonetheless, the poet has taken these numerous citations and collocated them into a well-crafted psalm that summons Yahweh's servants to praise him for his superiority over other gods and his tender care for his people.

One of the key aspects of this psalm's structure is its double inclusio: 1) hallelujah imperatives (vv. 1 and 21)[3] and 2) calls to praise/bless Yahweh (vv. 1–4 and 19–12). Verse 5, the first verse in the body of the psalm, sets the theme for the entire psalm, viz., the supremacy of Yahweh over other gods. Verses 6–12 recount Yahweh's ability to act in creation and his historical victories over other nations as evidences of his superiority. Because of these great acts, Yahweh is worthy of praise, so vv. 13–14 offer praise to Yahweh for his eternal renown demonstrated in his care for his people. Finally, the psalm's body concludes in vv. 15–18 with a polemic against the idols of the nations who are lifeless.

A Call to Praise Yahweh (vv. 1–4)

The delineation of the opening stanza of Ps 135 is somewhat difficult. There are three major options: 1) vv. 1–3; 2) vv. 1–4; and 3) vv. 1–5.[4] I have chosen

---

1. For a list of these intertextual references, see Hossfeld and Zenger, *Psalms*, 495.

2. Mathys, *Dichter und Beter*, 260. Author's translation of "Wenn auf einen Psalm die Bezeichnung 'Mosaik' zutrifft, dann auf Ps 135."

3. This is a common feature of many of the hallelujah psalms in the MT Psalter. See Barré, "Halelû yāh," 195.

4. For option one, see Gerstenberger, *Psalms, Part II, and Lamentations*, 377; Mays, *Psalms*, 415; and Ḥakham, *Psalms 101–150*, 369. For option three, see Terrien, *The Psalms*, 857 and Goldingay, *Psalms 90–150*, 578. The majority of commentators favor option two. For example, see McCann, *NIB*, 4:1219; Hossfeld and Zenger, *Psalms*, 493;

the second option (vv. 1–4) for several reasons. First, although v. 4 lacks a hallelujah command, this is not a suffient reason to exclude it from the opening stanza since v. 2 also lacks a hallelujah command. Thus, one can divide the stanza into two strophes. The first verse of each strophe (vv. 1, 3) begins with a command to praise and contains two imperatives. The second verse of the first strophe (v. 2) gives additional information about the "who" of the command whereas the second verse of the second strophe (v. 4) gives more details on the "why" of the praise command.

Second, several lexical and semantic features bind vv. 1–4 together. The first of these features is the threefold repetition of the divine name יה ("Yah") (vv. 1, 3, 4). These are the only three instances of this name in this psalm. A second feature is the positioning of a divine name at the end of all the first cola in vv. 1–4. A last feature that unites these verses is the covenant overtones in vv. 2 and 4. Verse 2 hints at the covenant relationship from the perspective of Yahweh's servants (אלהינו, "our God") and v. 4 outlines it from the divine perspective (סגלתו, "his possession").

Third, Ruth Scoralick has highlighted the symmetry of the frame (vv. 1–4 and 19–21), which is evident in the sevenfold use of God's name and the presence of five imperatives in each part of the frame.[5] A further connection between the two parts of the frame is the mention of Israel in last verse of the first part (v. 4) and the first verse of the second part (v. 19). Therefore, even though identifying vv. 1–3 as the opening stanza is attractive, it seems best to identify vv. 1–4 as the opening stanza and to divide it into two strophes (vv. 1–2 and 3–4).

Yahweh's Servants Are Summoned to Praise (vv. 1–2)

The opening verse of this psalm consists of an initial הללו יה ("hallelujah") (v. 1a)—identifying this psalm as one of the hallelujah psalms, which are limited to the fourth and fifth books of the Psalter—and a bi-colon (v. 1bc). It is almost identical to the opening verse of Ps 113, except that the order of the two cola is reversed in Ps 135:1.[6]

The bi-colon of v. 1bc repeats and expands the opening command. It has an accent count of 3 + 3, with each colon containing 12 consonants.

---

and Allen, *Psalms 101–150*, 290.

5. Scoralick, "Hallelujah," 255.

6. The reversal of the cola is probably due to the further explication of Yahweh's servants (v. 1) in v. 2.

This equal number of consonants may explain the "extras" in this bi-colon: 1) the direct object marker[7] and 2) the use of the metonymy שם יהוה ("the name of Yahweh") to refer to Yahweh.

Both cola begin with the command הללו ("praise") and end with the divine name יהוה ("Yahweh") (lexical parallelism). The differences between the two cola are associated with the middle element in each. Verse 1b gives the object of praise (שם יהוה, "the name of Yahweh") whereas v. 1c supplies the addressees of the command (עבדי יהוה, "servants of Yahweh").

The opening relative pronoun (ש) of v. 2 links v. 2 with v. 1c.[8] The purpose of this connection is to provide additional information about Yahweh's servants (v. 1c), namely, their location. The initial participle (עמדים) governs both cola and designates the posture of the servants, i.e., they are "standing." The second half of v. 2a and the entire second colon describe the place of their standing.

This bi-colon, like v. 1bc, has an accent count of 3 + 3.[9] On the lexical level, the ב ("in") preposition and the noun בית ("house") appear in both cola,[10] and the divine names at the end of each cola (יהוה ["Yahweh"] in v. 2a; אלהים ["God"] in v. 2b) parallel each other. On the semantic level, v. 2b specifies the location of the servants within the בית יהוה ("house of Yahweh").

The last word in v. 2b is significant for two reasons. First, this is the only place in this psalm where the psalmist calls Yahweh אלהים ("God"). Second, this is one of two instances of the 1cp pronoun in this psalm.[11] This possessive perspective parallels v. 1c, where the addressees are called Yahweh's servants. Accordingly, they are only able to refer to him as "our God" because he possesses them. Allen states that this "ushers in the covenant theme of the psalm," a theme that finds fuller expression in v. 4.[12]

The repetition of יהוה ("Yahweh") in v. 2a corresponds to the double appearance of this divine name in the first verse. In all three instances, it is in construct with its preceding noun (שם ["name"] in v. 1b; עבדי ["servants"]

---

7. The direct object marker only appears in three verses in Ps 135: vv. 1, 19, and 20.

8. This relative pronoun is limited to the fifth book of the Psalter.

9. Like the bi-colon of v. 1, the two cola of v. 2 almost have an identical letter count (14 x 15).

10. The repetition of these two lexemes contributes to the phonological parallelism in this verse: בבית (v. 2a), בחצרות (v. 2b), and בית (v. 2b).

11. The 1cp suffixed pronoun also appears in v. 5.

12. Allen, *Psalms 101–150*, 290.

in v. 1c; בית ["house"] in v. 2a). With these three nouns, there is a descending staircase from Yahweh's essence (שם) to his people (עבדי) to his place (בית).

Reasons for the Praise of Yahweh (vv. 3–4)

Verse 3 begins with a verbatim repetition of the command in v. 1a: הללו־יה ("hallelujah"). This verse is the only place in the Psalter where this command occurs outside of "the opening or closing phrase of a psalm. The line thus constitutes a resumed beginning of the psalm."[13] This "resumptive repetition" signals a shift in this first stanza.[14] The portrayal of the עבדי יהוה ("servants of Yahweh") is complete, and the author uses this repetition to bring his readers back to the theme of the opening verse, i.e., the necessity of praising Yahweh.

This bi-colon has an accent count of 3 + 4 and exhibits extensive parallelism. Lexically, כי ("for") is repeated in both cola.[15] Also, this bi-colon contains a few common word pairs (הלל/זמר ["praise"/"sing"], יה/שמו ["Yah"/"his name"], and טוב/נעים ["good"/"pleasant"]), all of which exhibit paradigmatic parallelism.[16] In the verb and adjective pairs, the more specific/poetic term occurs in the second colon.[17] The praising of Yahweh (הלל) in v. 3a is specified in v. 3b as making music to him (זמר). Yahweh's goodness (טוב) in v. 3a forms a pair with the primarily poetic term נעים ("pleasant") in v. 3b.[18]

The only anomaly in the lexical parallelism of these two cola is the presence of יהוה ("Yahweh") at the end of v. 3a. Not only does it lack a parallel in the second colon, but it is also not required for a proper understanding

---

13. Goldingay, *Psalms 90–150*, 579.

14. I have borrowed the phrase "resumptive repetition" from Alter, "Introduction," 28.

15. Kuntz ("Grounds for Praise," 162) identifies both the כי clauses in this verse, along with v. 4, as motive clauses.

16. Some examples of the word pairs are as follows: הלל/זמר–146:2; 149:3; שם/יה–v. 1; טוב/נעים–133:1; 147:1.

17. This is a common feature of Hebrew poetry, as noted by Alter, *Art*, 13.

18. Ḥakham, *Psalms 101–150*, 370. Alter (*Psalms*, 465) states that the pairing of זמר and נעים "is idiomatic in biblical Hebrew." Also, נעים most likely modifies שמו (cf. Allen, *Psalms 101–150*, 286).

of the colon.[19] Therefore, it is emphatic, leaving no doubt as to which noun טוב ("good") modifies.

The presence of the divine name at the end of v. 3a is also significant on the level of the stanza. First, v. 3a begins with the imperative הללו ("praise") and ends with the divine name יהוה ("Yahweh"). With such, it corresponds to v. 1bc. Second, its location at the end of the colon continues the rhyme between the initial cola of vv. 1–3. The first colon of each of these verses (v. 1b, 2a, 3a) ends with יהוה ("Yahweh") (the layout of BHS highlights this rhyme).

The opening כי ("for") of v. 4 builds on the two כי ("for") clauses of v. 3 by suppling an additional reason why Yahweh's servants should praise him (i.e., ground clause). He is worthy of praise because he chose Israel as "his possession" (סגלתו). This verse is almost a direct replication of several Pentateuchal passages (Exod 19:5; Deut 7:6; 14:2; 26:18). This 4 + 2 bicolon differs from v. 3, where almost every element of the first colon was matched in the second colon. In this verse, the components of v. 4b only correspond to two of the five words in v. 4a. The particle כי ("for"), the subject (יה ["Yah"]), and the verb (בחר ["chose"]) are all assumed in the second colon (i.e., gapping), serving double duty across the bi-colon.

Because of the brevity of v. 4b, the parallelism between these two cola is related to the direct objects and prepositional phrases in both cola. The word pair יעקב/ישראל ("Jacob"/"Israel") exhibits co-referentiality because both terms refer to the same group of people.[20] The ל ("for") prepositional phrases of the bi-colon also parallel one another (לו ["for himself"] in v. 4a; לסגלתו ["for his possession"] in v. 4b) and their relationship is one of intensification.[21] The term סגלה ("possession") only appears here in the Psalter and emphasizes the intimate and exclusive character of Yahweh's election of Israel. This emphasis moves the second colon one-step further than the first.

One of the anomalous features of v. 4a is the position of the divine name יה ("Yah").[22] As the last word of the colon, it follows a pronoun for which it is the antecedent. A possible explanation for this anastrophe is the

---

19. Hossfeld and Zenger (*Psalms*, 497) emphasize the importance of the formula כי טוב יהוה in "the postexilic Temple liturgy."

20. The label יעקב is a common "poetic designation of the Jewish people" (Ḥakham, *Psalms 101–150*, 370). This term occurs 34 times in the Psalter. When the word pair יעקב/ישראל occurs in the Psalter, יעקב is the first term more often.

21. This is a good example of Kugel's formula "A is so, what's more B" (*Idea*, 1).

22. This divine name appears primarily in the Psalter (43 of its 49 occurences).

pattern within this stanza in which the first colon of each verse concludes with a divine name. As previously noted, vv. 1b, 2a, and 3a all end with יהוה ("Yahweh"). In this regard, v. 4a is different (because it has יה ["Yah"]), but nonetheless the peculiar position of יה ("Yah") appears to be motivated by such a pattern.

Verse 4a also has strong connections with v. 2b. The relationship between these two cola revolves around the verb בחר ("chose") in v. 4a. This verb displays both semantic and phonological (בחצרות ["in the courts"] [v. 2b] and בחר ["chose"] [v. 4a]) parallels with v. 2b. In the previous analysis of v. 2b, I highlighted the covenant overtones associated with אלהינו ("our God"). Such a covenant perspective is the primary feature of v. 4. Particularly, בחר ("to choose") often describes Yahweh's initiative in his covenant relationship with Jacob/Israel.[23] Thus, he is their God (v. 2b) only because he chose them (v. 4a) as his prized possession (v. 4b). This covenant language also builds on the servant language of v. 1c.

Yahweh's Superiority over All Gods (vv. 5–18)

The body of Ps 135 highlights Yahweh's superiority over all other gods, a theme introduced in the first verse of the body (v. 5). The separation of v. 5 from the introductory stanza (vv. 1–4) and its subsequent inclusion in the psalm's main body is based on three factors: 1) the switch to first person, 2) several emphatic components (discussed below) and 3) its importance in setting the theme for the remainder of the body of the psalm.[24] At the other end of the body, the break between vv. 18 and 19 is apparent because of the resumption of the call to praise in vv. 19–21.

On a broad level, the body of this psalm possesses a chiastic structure. Verses 5–12 are about what Yahweh can do while vv. 15–18 are about what the idols cannot do.[25] Between these two larger sections is a doxological interruption (vv. 13–14), which is the focal point the body's structure.

---

23. Compare Ps 135:4 with Deut 7:6 and 14:2.

24. Lugt (*Cantos and Strophes*, 79) states that the personal pronoun אני ("I") "primarily denote[s] the beginning of a strophe." Muilenburg ("Form Criticism and Beyond," 39) names "shifts ... of the speaker" as one of the markers of a break or turning point in poetry.

25. Alden, "Chiastic Psalms," 207.

Part 1: The Poetry of Psalms 135–137

Yahweh's Superior Greatness (vv. 5–6)

There are two reasons why I have differentiated vv. 5–6 as a stanza. First, the topics of these two verses are broader than the subject matter of vv. 7–12. These two verses set the tone for the specific examples of vv. 7–12. Specifically, v. 5 provides the overarching theme of the entire section, and v. 6 gives the primary proof of Yahweh's superiority. Second, after v. 6 Yahweh is not explicitly named until v. 13. Each new strophe in the second stanza of the body (vv. 7–12) references Yahweh with either a participle (v. 7) or relative pronoun (vv. 8 & 10).

Yahweh's Superior Greatness (v. 5)

This verse is almost a direct citation of Exod 18:11, which is part of Jethro's blessing of Yahweh for his deliverance of Israel from the Egyptians. The initial issue in an analysis of this verse is whether it is a bi-colon or tri-colon. The editors of BHS present it as a bi-colon with an accent count of 5 + 2. However, one could as easily classify it as a tri-colon with an accent count of 3 + 2 + 2.[26] I classify it as a tri-colon because of its close relationship with v. 6 and the paucity of a five accent colon in Hebrew poetry.

The entire first colon serves as a marker of emphasis. The psalmist could have begun the verse with the second colon and conveyed his message adequately. However, by including v. 5a, the psalmist has highlighted the contents of his knowledge (v. 5bc). The prominence of this first colon is apparent in a couple of ways. First, v. 5a is distinguished by the switch to the first person singular.[27] Second, the first two words of v. 5a are emphatic. Although the כי ("indeed") that opens this verse is the fourth כי of the psalm, this instance of the particle differs from the first three in that it does not introduce a motive clause but emphatically highlights the contents of this verse.[28] The second word of v. 5, the 1cs personal pronoun אני ("I"), is also emphatic since the first person subject is signified by the verb ידעתי ("I know").

---

26. The near context of the verse supports either option. For instance, v. 4 is a bi-colon with an accent count of 4 + 2 (supports the former option). In contrast, v. 6 is a tri-colon with an accent count of 3 + 3 + 2.

27. This is the only instance of the 1cs in this psalm.

28. Ḥakham, *Psalms 101–150*, 370. Kraus (*Psalms 60–150*, 493) calls it "an affirmative כי."

The parallelism between the first two cola is syntagmatic since v. 5b provides the content of the psalmist's knowledge. The lexical correspondence between these cola is limited to the repetition of כי ("indeed" or "that") as the initial word of each colon; however, the second כי ("that") introduces the content of the psalmist's knowledge and thus serves a different grammatical function.

The second and third cola also exhibit syntagmatic parallelism because v. 5c introduces a contrast between Yahweh and all other gods. Yet, the psalmist links these final two cola by means of the comparison that extends across them.[29] The comparison between אדנינו ("our Lord") and כל־אלהים ("all gods") in v. 5c is contingent upon the adjective גדול ("great") in v. 5b (i.e. it serves double duty). Thus, v. 5c provides additional information about the greatness of Yahweh, namely, his greatness surpasses that of all other gods.

In addition, v. 5b and c parallel each other lexically through their divine designations. The psalmist identifies Yahweh (v. 5b) as אדנינו ("our Lord") in v. 5c. This move from יהוה ("Yahweh") to אדנינו ("our Lord") corresponds to a similar clarification in v. 2 where יהוה ("Yahweh") (v. 2a) is identified as אלהינו ("our God") (v. 2b). These cola (vv. 2b and 5c) are the only two places where the 1cp pronominal suffix appears in this psalm, and v. 5c marks the only occurrence of אדון ("Lord") in this psalm.[30] Another parallel between these verses is the presence of אלהים ("god") in v. 5c and v. 2b. In v. 2 its referent is Yahweh, but here it refers to all other gods.[31] This parallel simply reinforces the obvious contrast already present in v. 5.

Another parallel between this verse and an earlier verse is between the כי clauses of v. 5b (כי־גדול יהוה ["that Yahweh is great"]) and v. 3a (כי־טוב יהוה ["for Yahweh is good"]). His goodness (v. 3a) is explained with reference to his relationship with his people and his greatness (v. 5b) in contrast to all other gods. These two adjectives highlight two major themes of the psalm. However, these themes are not completely distinct because the proof of his goodness toward his people (vv. 4, 13–14) is often visible in his displays of greatness over other gods (vv. 8–12).

---

29. Watson (*Classical*, 157) identifies this verse as an example of "synonymous-sequential parallelism," as explained in Miller, "Synonymous-Sequential Parallelism," 256–60.

30. This divine name is rare in the Psalter, only appearing 13 times. Six of these 13 occurrences are in Book V of the Psalter and three of these six are in Pss 135–136.

31. Later in the psalm, the psalmist identifies these gods as עצבי הגוים (v. 15).

Part 1: The Poetry of Psalms 135–137

Primary Proof of Yahweh's Superior Greatness: Freedom to Act as He Pleases (v. 6)

Verse 6 builds on the theme of v. 5 by giving the primary proof of Yahweh's superior greatness, i.e., his freedom to act according to his own pleasure in every part of his creation.[32] It is a tri-colon with an accent count of 3 + 3 + 2. The opening verb of the second colon (עשׂה ["does"]) is the main verb of the tri-colon.[33] Verse 6a supplies its subject and object while the rest of v. 6b and v. 6c contain adverbial prepositional phrases that identify the spheres of Yahweh's action. In addition, a simple comparison of the verbs in the first two cola (חפץ ["desires"] in v. 6a; עשׂה ["does"] in v. 6b) elucidates the semantic progression (i.e., syntagmatic parallelism) between these two cola. There is a move from inward desire (חפץ) to outward expression (עשׂה).

After the opening verb of v. 6b, the rest of the second colon and the entire third colon consist of a list of places where Yahweh's actions are visible. The four places listed in these two cola represent what Berlin has termed "conventionalized coordinates."[34] Ḥakham has noted that within this list there is a descent from the highest to the lowest regions of the world (heavens → earth → sea → the depths).[35] Such a complete description is not essential (cf. Ps 115:3), but this merism emphasizes the totality of the created order and parallels the totality (כל ["all"]) of Yahweh's desires in the first colon. All his delights (v. 6a) find expression in every part of creation (v. 6bc).

A closer examination of the four places of v. 6bc reveals that the psalmist has divided creation into two major spheres: 1) a non-aquatic sphere (v. 6b) and 2) an aquatic sphere (v. 6c).[36] Each sphere has a higher level (בשׁמים ["in the heavens"] in v. 6b and בימים ["in the seas"] in v. 6c) and a lower level (בארץ ["in the earth"] in v. 6b and כל־תהומות ["all the deeps"] in v. 6c). Several parallels between these two cola confirm this understanding. First, Watson cites these two cola as examples of "gender-matched parallelism" because the first place in each cola is masculine and

---

32. The first five words of this verse are almost identical to Ps 115:3.
33. The other verb (חפץ) is part of a subordinate אשׁר clause.
34. Berlin, *Dynamics*, 76.
35. Ḥakham, *Psalms 101–150*, 371.
36. Auffret, "Ton nom pour toujours," 233.

the second is feminine.[37] Second, the first items (i.e., the higher levels) lack the conjunction ו ("and"), whereas the second items (i.e., the lower levels) have it.[38] This asyndeton at the beginning of v. 6c produces alliteration (ב) between the two pairs. Finally, the first locations (i.e., the higher levels) in both cola resonate phonologically through the מים-x-ב sequence (בשמים in v. 6b; בימים in v. 6c). In fact, these two words only differ by one consonant.

In addition to its parallels with v. 6b, v. 6c connects back to v. 6a by means of the adjective כל ("all").[39] Its presence in the last accentual unit of v. 6 creates an inclusio around the entire tri-colon. This inclusio further underscores the comprehensive nature of God's desires and actions.

The twofold appearance of כל ("all") in v. 6 also serves as the key link to v. 5. In v. 5, כל ("all") is in the last accentual unit and modifies the gods whom Yahweh is greater than. Its position at the end of v. 5 and the beginning of v. 6 serves as a hinge between these two verses and reinforces their thematic relationship. Furthermore, the position of כל ("all") at the head of v. 6 also produces alliteration with vv. 4–5. Each of these verses begins with the consonant כ. Moreover, the presence of יהוה ("Yahweh") at the end of v. 6a continues the pattern that began in v. 1 of the psalmist ending the first colon of each verse with a divine name.[40]

Specific Examples of Yahweh's Superior Greatness (vv. 7–12)

After affirming Yahweh's freedom to do as he desires, the psalmist gives specific examples of how Yahweh demonstrates this in his creation. This stanza consists of three strophes. The first strophe (v. 7) describes Yahweh's control of his created order, the second strophe (vv. 8–12) describes Yahweh's destruction of the Egyptians (vv. 8–9), and the third strophe describes his destruction of the kings on the east and west of the Jordan (vv. 10–12).

---

37. Watson, *Classical*, 123.

38. The absence of this conjunction before בשמים ("in the heavens") is expected, but its absence before בימים ("in the seas") is significant since the psalmist could have placed the conjunction here.

39. The presence of this lexeme in v. 6c is an oddity since it does not appear with any of the other three places in v. 6bc.

40. The only exception to this pattern is v. 5, where the second colon ends with a divine name. Watson (*Classical*, 336–337) classifies v. 6a as an example of "delayed identification" because the subject (יהוה) is at the end of the colon. Such a delay may have been due to this pattern.

Part 1: The Poetry of Psalms 135–137

Two features distinguish this stanza from the stanzas that bracket it. First, the divine name is absent from these verses even though Yahweh is the subject of every verse.[41] Second, there is a pattern associated with the type of verses (i.e., bi-colon vs. tri-colon) in this stanza. Of the six verses, three are tri-cola and three are bi-cola. These two types are arranged in an alternating fashion moving from tri-colon to bi-colon three times.

Yahweh's Crafting of Storms (v. 7)

Verse 7 is almost identical to two verses in Jeremiah (10:13 and 51:16), both of which appear in contexts dealing with Yahweh's distinctiveness in contrast to idols. This verse is a tri-colon with an accent count of 4 + 3 + 2 and has strong parallels on the syntactical, morphological, and phonological levels.[42] The lexical and semantic parallelism is syntagmatic since the verse is a catalogue of the different aspects of a Yahweh-produced thunderstorm. All the nouns fall under Berlin's category of "normal syntagmatic connections" since all these words commonly appear in ordinary discourse revolving around storms.[43] The direct objects are "three things that accompany rain"[44] and the three prepositional objects represent different components of Yahweh's creation.

On the semantic level, v. 7b is exceptional. In v. 7a and c, Yahweh's action is connected with another source (in both instances, this is highlighted by the preposition מִן ["from"]).[45] In contrast, such an intermediary source is not included in v. 7b, where Yahweh himself is the source of lighting.

---

41. The subject of every verb in vv. 7–12 is the divine name in v. 6.

42. Syntactically, all three verses are analogous (verb-direct object-prepositional phrase). On the morphological level, the first two cola have the most in common. The single morphological commonality between v. 7a and 7c is the hiphil participle in each. Hossfeld and Zenger (*Psalms,* 498) and Scoralick ("Hallelujah," 256) identify one of the purposes of these two participles as preparation of the Exodus theme in the next verse.
The phonological parallels are as follows: מקצה (v. 7a) and ברקים (v. 7b). Verse 7c has strong internal phonological parallelism between מוצא־רוח and מאוצרותיו. Ḥakham (*Psalms 101–150,* 371–72) identifies this as "a play on words."

43. Berlin, *Dyanmics,* 77.

44. Ḥakham, *Psalms 101–150,* 371.

45. In v. 7a he brings clouds up "from the end of the earth" (מקצה הארץ). In v. 7c he brings out rain "from his/its storehouses" (מאוצרותיו). Cf. Goldingay, *Psalms 90–150,* 581.

Poetic Analysis of Psalm 135

Two lexical connections between vv. 6 and 7 confirm that v. 7 is a specific example of Yahweh's freedom to act (v. 6).[46] First, the verb עשׂה ("does" or "makes") only appears three times in this psalm. Two of these three occurrences are found in vv. 6 and 7.[47] In both verses, it appears in the center colon. The second lexical connection between vv. 6 and 7 is the repetition of the lexeme ארץ ("earth") in vv. 6b and 7a. Both of these parallels reinforce the semantic relationship of these two verses. Yahweh's bringing of clouds from the end of the earth (v. 7a) and his making of lighting (v. 7b) are specific examples of his freedom to act according to his pleasure in the heavens and the earth (v. 6b).

Yahweh's Historical Victories (vv. 8–12)

With v. 8 the psalmist turns his attention from Yahweh's control over one aspect of his creation to his actions against other nations and their kings.[48] His works in Egypt are the topic of vv. 8–9; vv. 10–12 move to Yahweh's defeat of the kings on the east and west side of the Jordan and his gift of their land as an inheritance to his people. Noticeably absent from this "rapid poetic summary of God's triumphant acts"[49] is any mention of Yahweh's rescue of his people from Egypt,[50] the Passover, or the events surrounding Sinai and the giving of the Mosaic Covenant.[51]

The bi-colon of v. 8, which is a summary of Exod 12:29, has an accent count of 3 + 2 and is characterized by syntagmatic parallelism.[52] The second colon specifies the direct object of the first colon (בכורי מצרים ["firstborn of Egypt"]) as the firstborn of both man and beast.

In contrast to v. 8, which deals with the last and greatest plague in Egypt,[53] v. 9 zooms out and focuses on all the plagues with which God tar-

---

46. Ḥakham (*Psalms 101–150*, 371) writes, "Everything mentioned in this verse is an example of what was stated in the previous verse."

47. The third instance of this verb is in v. 18.

48. Hossfeld and Zenger (*Psalms*, 498) connect this abrupt transition to an assumption of the history of Israel "as portrayed in the Pentateuch."

49. Alter, *Psalms*, 466.

50. Hossfeld and Zenger, *Psalms*, 498.

51. Terrien, *The Psalms*, 858.

52. The parallels between the two cola of this verse are primarily on the phonological level: מצרים (v. 8a) and מאדם (v. 8b). מצרים (v. 8a) resonates with מאוצרותיו (v. 7).

53. Barnes, *Notes*, 275.

geted the Egyptians.⁵⁴ This poetic paraphrase of Deut 34:11 is a tri-colon with an accent count of 3 + 2 + 2. The three cola of v. 9 display syntagmatic parallelism. Verse 9a gives the main action of the verse (שׁלח ["sent"]). Based on the relative pronoun in v. 8, the understood subject of this verb is Yahweh. The objects of the verb (אתות ומפתים ["signs and wonders"]) often appear together in summaries of the plagues, especially in Deuteronomy.⁵⁵

The last two cola give additional information regarding Yahweh's actions. Verse 9b identifies the arena in which the action of v. 9a takes place (מצרים ["Egypt"]) and contains the "unusual expression" בתוככי ("in the midst").⁵⁶ Verse 9c names the specific targets of Yahweh's action: בפרעה ובכל־עבדיו ("against Pharaoh and all his servants").

The only lexical parallel in this tri-colon is the threefold repetition of the ב ("in" or "against") preposition in v. 9b and c, which results in a semantic contrast between the first ב ("in") (v. 9b) and the other two ("against") (v. 9c). The former marks location while the latter two are "adversative."⁵⁷ Moreover, the repetition of ב at the beginning of v. 9b and c produces alliteration between these cola. This alliteration balances the rhyme between the first two cola (ומפתים [v. 9a] and מצרים [v. 9b]).

On the level of the psalm, this verse has several parallels with previous verses. First, the initial שׁ (שׁלח ["sent"]) of v. 9 is part of an alliteration chain that is related to the initial morpheme of vv. 8–10.⁵⁸ Second, the mention of מצרים ("Egypt") in v. 9b is a replication of the same term in v. 8a. Third, the adjective כל ("all") recalls the comprehensiveness of Yahweh's actions in vv. 5–6 (three occurrences of this adjective). Fourth, the lexeme עבדיו ("his servants") in v. 9c sets up a contrast with the עבדי יהוה ("servants of Yahweh") in v. 1. The irony of this contrast is that one of the reasons why

54. The motivation for this arrangement might have been the psalmist's desire to begin both stophes (vv. 8–9 and vv. 10–12) with the same phrase (שׁהכה).

55. Hossfeld and Zenger (*Psalms*, 498) cite Deut 6:22; 26:8; 29:2; 34:11.

56. Goldingay, *Psalms 90–150*, 582. The only other instance of this phrase is Ps 116:19. Some, such as Augustine (*Expositions*, 530) understand the ending of this word (כי) as the 2fs suffixed pronoun and translate the phrase "into the midst of thee." In contrast, Allen (*Psalms 101–150*, 286) writes, "A second-person address would be out of place here." With Allen, I identify it as "a poetic substitute for the word" בתוך (Ḥakham, *Psalms 101–150*, 372).

57. Waltke and O'Connor, *Biblical Hebrew Syntax*, 197.

58. The likelihood that this phonological resonance may have been one of the factors in the psalmist's selection of שׁלח as the verb is heightened when one considers that this is the only place where this verb is used to describe Yahweh's action in reference to the "signs and wonders."

Poetic Analysis of Psalm 135

"Yahweh's servants" are commanded to praise Yahweh is because he sent his plagues against the "servants of Pharaoh."

Verse 10 marks a transition in the stanza from Yahweh's actions against one nation and its king to Yahweh's destruction of many nations and their kings. This bi-colon has an accent count of 3 + 3 and demonstrates pervasive parallelism. The fourfold repetition (twice in each colon) of the masculine singular ending -ים produces rhyme across the two cola.

Lexically, the two verbs (נכה ["strike"] and הרג ["kill"]) are synonyms. Although the first verb (נכה ["strike"]) can appear in a non-fatal or fatal context,[59] the context of this verse is clearly fatal. The word pair גוים/מלכים ("nations"/"kings") (the direct objects) is an example of a correlative word pair since מלכים ("kings") is usually associated with גוים ("nations").[60] In this context, the kings serve as representatives of their respective nations. The adjectives that conclude both cola (רבים/עצומים ["many"/"mighty"]) are a common word pair most often used to describe peoples (עמים) or nations (גוים).[61] The coupling of these adjectives draws out two aspects of greatness: number (רב) and might (עצום).[62] Therefore, Yahweh struck many nations who had mighty kings.

The most significant connection between v. 10 and earlier verses is the initial שהכה ("who struck"), which also appears at the beginning of v. 8. This repetition correlates Yahweh's actions against one sector of Egyptian society (i.e., the firstborn) with his action against the kings and nations who stood in the way of his people.[63] This repetition also completes the aforementioned alliteration between vv. 8–10.

Furthermore, the four appearances of the masculine singular ending -ים parallel the double appearance of this consonant pair in v. 9. In fact, the presence of this pair doubles in each verse moving from v. 8 to v. 10 to form a crescendo. It appears once in v. 8 (מצרים), twice in v. 9 (ומפתים and מצרים), and four times in v. 10 (גוים, רבים, מלכים, and עצומים). The position of this phoneme pair in each of these verses is even more significant. It appears at the end of the first colon of each of these verses (vv. 8–10), thus creating a

---

59. BDB, 645–46. HALOT 2:698–99.
60. Watson, *Classical*, 132.
61. This is the only place where עצום modifies מלך.
62. Cf. BDB, 783, 912–13; HALOT 3:1171–1173, 2:869.
63. Both Hossfeld and Zenger (*Psalms*, 499) and Goldingay (*Psalms 90–150*, 582) point out that this viewpoint differs from the narratives of Numbers, Deuteronomy, and Joshua, which do not speak directly of Yahweh striking Og, Sihon, and the other kingdoms.

vertical rhyme across the three verses. Moreover, it concludes the first and second cola of vv. 9–10, thus creating even more rhyme (between vv. 9ab and 10ab). These phonological parallels, along with the repetition of שהכה, fasten these two strophes (vv. 8–9 & vv. 10–12) together securely.

Verse 11 continues v. 10 by identifying two of the kings and a particular set of kingdoms that Yahweh struck.[64] The three lamed prepositions link each colon to the verbs of v. 10. Verse 11 is a tri-colon with an accent count of 3 + 3 + 3. The first two cola are almost identical because they list the two kings (Sihon and Og) Moses defeated and the people on the east of the Jordan. These kings frequently appear together in the OT and are therefore "conventionalized coordinates."[65] The third colon differs in a couple of ways from the first two: 1) it references kingdoms instead of kings and 2) it shifts the focus to Joshua's conquest of the west-Jordanian kingdoms.

As with the subject matter, the parallelism between the first two cola is the strongest. On the lexical level, this tri-cola demonstrates paradigmatic parallelism. All the words within v. 11a and b parallel each other: 1) the lamed prepositions, 2) the names of the kings (סיחון ["Sihon"] and עוג ["Og"]), 3) the word מלך ("king"), and 4) the names of their kingdoms (האמרי ["the Amorites"] and הבשן ["Bashan"]). Verse 11c parallels the first two cola in two ways: 1) the lamed preposition and 2) the designation of the location of the kingdoms (כנען ["Canaan"]). The phonological parallels—מלך ("king") in v. 11a and b resonates with ממלכות ("kingdoms") in v. 11c and ולכל ("and all") in v. 11c—build upon and reinforce the lexical links between the cola.

The multiple connections within the present section (vv. 8–12) continue with v. 11. On the lexical level, the two instances of the singular מלך ("king") (v. 11a and b) correspond to the plural מלכים ("kings") in v. 10b, while ממלכות ("kingdoms") in v. 11c is synonymous with גוים ("nations") in v. 10a. These two parallels show that there is a switch in the objects of vv. 10–11. In v. 10, the verbal objects move from general (גוים ["nations"]) to specific (מלכים ["kings"]), but the objects of v. 11 move from specific (סיחון ["Sihon"] and עוג ["Og"]) to general (כל ממלכות כנען ["all the kingdoms of Canaan"]), thus establishing a chiastic pattern between these two verses (ab/b′a′).[66]

---

64. Delitzsch (*Commentary*, 326) links this verse to Deut 3:21.
65. Berlin, *Dynamics*, 76.
66. Allen, *Psalms 101–150*, 287.

POETIC ANALYSIS OF PSALM 135

In addition to these links with v. 10, v. 11 also has ties with vv. 8–9. The presence of specific names of kings (סיחון ["Sihon"] and עוג ["Og"]) and the location of kingdoms (כנען ,הבשן, האמרי ["the Amorites," "Bashan," and "Canaan"]) in v. 11 correspond to the name of a king (פרעה ["Pharaoh"]) and his kingdom (מצרים ["Egypt"]) in vv. 8–9. Auffret notes that vv. 8 and 11 give the "starting point (Egypt) and arrival point (Canaan) of the Exodus."[67] Furthermore, the כל ("all") of v. 11c matches the same adjective in v. 9c. Just as "all" the servants of Pharaoh were the object of Yahweh's plagues (v. 9), so "all" the kingdoms of Canaan are the object of Yahweh's striking (v. 11).

So far, the psalmist's tour through Yahweh's historical acts (vv. 8–12) has only highlighted his actions against enemy nations. This pattern ceases with v. 12. In this partial citation of Deut 4:38,[68] the psalmist draws attention to Yahweh's favorable actions toward Israel, even at the expense of these other kings and kingdoms. In particular, his ability to give their land to his people further demonstrates his greatness over all other gods. Even though this verse switches directions in some respects, it is closely related to vv. 10–11 by the initial ו ("and") and the 3mp pronominal suffix in v. 12a (ארצם ["their land"]), the antecedents of which are the kings and kingdoms of vv. 10–11.

This verse is a bi-colon with an accent count of 3 + 3. With the exception of the repetition of נחלה ("inheritance") at the beginning of v. 12b, the verse reads like an indicative sentence. Verse 12a contains the verb (נתן ["give"]), the direct object (ארצם ["their land"]), and a modifying noun (נחלה ["inheritance"]). After a repetition of this last noun, v. 12b gives the indirect object (לישראל ["to Israel"]). The last word of the verse (עמו ["his people"]) stands in apposition to ישראל ("Israel") and specifies Yahweh's particular relationship with them.

Due to the nature of this verse, only a few parallels between the cola are present, the most important of which is the anadiplosis in this verse (repetition of נחלה ["inheritance"]). This is the only lexical parallel between the cola and serves as a marker of emphasis.[69] Hence, the stress is not so

---

67. Auffret, "Ton nom pour toujours," 228. Author's translation of "point de départ (Égypte) et point d'arrivé (Canaan) de l'exode."

68. Delitzsch, *Commentary*, 326.

69. Goldingay, *Psalms 90–150*, 582. Anderson (*Psalms 73–150*, 892) states that this repetition is "a poetical device and it stresses the new significance of the one-time 'kingdoms of Canaan.'"

25

much on the gift itself (ארצם ["their land"]) nor on the recipients (ישראל עמו ["Israel his people"]), but on the nature of the gift (נחלה ["inheritance"]).

Before this verse, the last reference to Israel was in v. 4. Moreover, the last place where the 3msp suffixed pronoun was used with Yahweh as its antecedent (as in v. 12) was in v. 4 (where it appears twice). These parallels between vv. 4 and 12 are significant. Verse 4 is the final verse of the opening call to praise and v. 12 is the final verse of the present section, which deals with Yahweh's historical actions against other nations (vv. 8–12).[70] Both verses highlight Yahweh's special relationship with the people of Israel. In v. 4, he chose them for himself as his סגלה ("possession"). In v. 12, they are his people to whom he gives the land as a נחלה ("inheritance").[71] The close semantic relationship between these two terms sets up a comparison between Yahweh's possession of Israel and Israel's possession of the land. Since Yahweh chose Israel as his special possession, he gave them the land as a precious possession (i.e., an inheritance).

The reference to Israel as עמו ("his people") also parallels the designation of Yahweh as אלהינו ("our God") (v. 2) and אדנינו ("our Lord") (v. 5) earlier in the psalm. The 3ms pronoun of v. 12 and the 1cp pronouns of vv. 2 and 5 represent the two sides of the covenant relationship between Yahweh and Israel. Because he is their God, they praise him; because they are his people, he defeated their adversaries and gave their land to Israel.

Confession of Yahweh's Eternal Renown (vv. 13–14)

Several factors indicate that v. 13 marks a crevice in this psalm. First, the initial vocative address to יהוה ("Yahweh") (v. 13) is the only direct speech to Yahweh in the psalm. Such a sudden direct speech to Yahweh is a standard signal of a new strophe.[72] Second, and closely related, the three incidents of the divine name יהוה ("Yahweh") in vv. 13–14 are the first specific references to Yahweh since v. 6. Third, vv. 8–12 re-narrated Yahweh's *past* actions, but vv. 13–14 turn the reader's attention to the *present* and *future* (לעולם ["to forever"] and לדר־ודר ["from generation to generation"] in v.

---

70. Fokkelman (*Major Poems*, 2:299) writes, "The parallelism of vv.4 [sic] and 12 exceeds strophe level by marking the ends of stanzas I and II."

71. Fokkelman (*Major Poems*, 2:299) identifies נחלה (v. 12) and סגלה (v. 4) as synonyms.

72. Fokkelman, *Major Poems*, 2:299; Muilenburg, "Form Criticism and Beyond," 42; Lugt, *Cantos and Strophes*, 79.

Poetic Analysis of Psalm 135

13). Fourth, vv. 7–12 described specific actions of Yahweh whereas v. 13 (and v. 14) is far more general.

Praise for Yahweh's Eternal Renown (v. 13)

Verse 13 is a quotation of Yahweh's instructions to Moses in Exod 3:15, in which Yahweh describes himself to Moses (Exod 3:13). In this verse (Ps 135:13), the psalmist takes Yahweh's words and uses them as his own words of praise to Yahweh. This doxology[73] was no doubt prompted by the rehearsal of Yahweh's actions in vv. 7–12[74] and shows "that he is now as he was in these events."[75]

This verse is a bi-colon with an accent count of 3 + 3 and contains extensive parallelism. Semantically, both cola are alike, focusing on the perpetuity of Yahweh's renown. On the lexical level, the most obvious parallel is the repetition of the divine name at the beginning of both cola. It is only appropriate that the divine name appears twice in a verse stating that his "name" endures forever. The second lexical parallel is the word pair שמך/זכרך ("your name"/"your remembrance"). In this pair, the second noun (זכר ["remembrance"]) clarifies the exact nature of the first (שם ["name"]).[76] Even though שם ("name") often appears as a metonymy for Yahweh himself, here it refers specifically to his reputation that will endure forever.[77] In the context of this psalm, his reputation is no doubt connected to the great historical acts recalled in vv. 8–12. The last lexical parallel is between the synonymous phrases at the end of each cola (לעולם ["to forever"] in v. 13a and לדר־ודר ["from generation to generation"] in v. 13b).[78]

Most of this verse's parallels with previous verses are associated with the first six verses of the psalm. On a very broad level, the doxological nature of this verse is an answer to the praise commands of the introduction. After reviewing Yahweh's great works, the psalmist himself cannot help but to participate in what he has commanded Yahweh's servants to do. Such a thematic similarity is reinforced by a couple of lexical correspondences.

---

73. Mathys, *Dichter und Beter*, 261.
74. Allen, *Psalms 101–150*, 291.
75. Barnes, *Notes*, 275.
76. The synonymy of the other two word pairs in this verse influences the close (synonymous) association of these two terms.
77. BDB (271) cites this verse as an example of זכר having a meaning similar to שם.
78. Ibid., 189.

First, the presence of the divine name resumes the trend of vv. 1–6, where at least one divine name appears in each verse. Second, the reference to Yahweh's שׁם ("name") in v. 13a links this verse to the two occurrences of this lexeme in vv. 1 and 3.

Reason for Yahweh's Eternal Renown: His Care for His People (v. 14)

The psalmist's use of Pentateuchal passages continues in v. 14 with a quotation of Deut 32:36. This bi-colon has an accent count of 3 + 2 and is bound to the previous verse by means of the כי ("for") that introduces this verse as a motive clause. In contrast to v. 13, the psalmist switches back to the third person in v. 14. Like v. 13, v. 14 has a timeless perspective.[79] Consequently, Yahweh's renown (v. 13) is intricately related to his work on behalf of his people (v. 14).[80] The move from praise (v. 13) to a motive clause about Yahweh's care for his people (v. 14) mirrors the same pattern in vv. 3–4.[81]

The parallels between the two cola are extensive.[82] On the lexical level, both cola have one word (not including the opening כי ["for"]) that is unique. The divine name יהוה ("Yahweh") in v. 14a is not repeated in v. 14b, serving double duty across the bi-colon. In v. 14b, the preposition על ("on") is exceptional. Its uniqueness is due to the nature of the verb in this colon and is, therefore, not semantically significant.[83]

The lexical parallels involve the two verbs and the two objects.[84] The verb in the first colon (דין) has several possible connotations: 1) positive (i.e., avenge), 2) neutral (i.e., govern), or 3) negative (i.e., execute judgment).[85] Within the context of Ps 135 and its focus on Yahweh's care for his people, the third of these does not appear to be an option. The parallel verb in v. 14b helps in properly adducing which of the first two best fits the present

---

79. This may explain the use of yiqtol verbs here.
80. Goulder (*Psalms of the Return*, 217) refers to v. 14 as "the heart of the psalm."
81. McCann, *NIB*, 4:1220.
82. Excluding the initial כי (v. 14a) and the ו at the beginning of v. 14b, every word begins with either a י or an ע. In v. 14a, one ע-initial word follows two י-initial words. The reverse occurs in v. 14b where one י-initial word follows two ע-initial words. Consequently, the three י-initial words bracket the three ע-initial words.
83. This preposition often governs the object of נחם. See BDB, 637–38.
84. The two objects are co-referents.
85. BDB, 192.

context. The second verb (נחם ["has compassion"]) has extremely positive connotations, so it is probably best to take the first option.[86] Yahweh's judgment of his people in this verse would point toward him avenging their enemies.[87] Such a meaning resounds with the theme of the previous verses (vv. 8–12).

The semantic relationship between the two cola is one of action-motive. Yahweh's compassion for his servants is what motivates his action of avenging them.[88] The presence of the 3ms suffix in each colon explains why he takes such an action toward them, i.e., they are *his*.

On the level of the psalm, several words in this verse parallel previous verses. First, the divine name יהוה ("Yahweh") hearkens back to its two appearances in the previous verse. These three appearances of יהוה ("Yahweh") set these two verses (vv. 13–14) apart from the preceding and following stanzas. Second, עמו ("his people") in v. 14a also appears in v. 12b in apposition to ישראל ("Israel"). The location of these two appearances bracket the doxological confession of v. 13 with a focus on Yahweh's past (v. 12) and present care (v. 14) for his people. Third, the mention of עבדיו ("his servants") in the second colon connects back to vv. 1 and 9. In v. 9 this same noun and suffixed pronoun refer to Pharaoh's servants who were the objects of Yahweh's plagues. In contrast, Yahweh's servants are the recipients of his compassion (v. 14) and are thus commanded to offer him praise (v. 1).

A Polemic against Idols and Their Worshippers (vv. 15–18)

The opening words of v. 15 introduce a new subject, viz., the idols of the nations. Thematically, these verses contrast with vv. 5–12.[89] The lifeless idols that do absolutely nothing are no match for Yahweh's great and free actions (vv. 5–12). These verses are very similar to Ps 115:4–6, 8, the context of which is almost identical to that of Ps 135.[90]

---

86. The translation "have compassion" (Anderson, *Psalms 73–150*, 892; Allen, *Psalms 101–150*, 286) is preferable to the more reflexive translation "relent" (Ḥakham, *Psalms 101–150*, 373), "repent himself" (Hengstenberg, *Commentary*, 474), or "gets himself relief" (Goldingay, *Psalms 90–150*, 583).

87. Cf. Allen, *Psalms 101–150*, 291.

88. Goldingay, *Psalms 90–150*, 583, writes, "'governs' is an action word and 'gets himself relief' is a feelings word."

89. Cohen, *The Psalms*, 494.

90. I will note the differences in my discussion of v. 17 (below).

The bi-colon of v. 15 has an accent count of 4 + 3. The opening noun phrase, עצבי הגוים ("idols of the nations"), serves as the subject of both cola (as well as the entire strophe). The parallels between the two cola are between the last two words of v. 15a and the entire second colon, since both serve as predicate nominatives of the subject. The two items at the end of v. 15a (כסף וזהב ["silver and gold"]) designate the material by which the idols are made, while v. 15b focuses on the human origin of these idols (מעשה ידי אדם ["work of human hands"]).

This verse has several parallels with other verses in the psalm. First, the word הגוים ("the nations") in v. 15a connects with the only other appearance of this word in the psalm (v. 10). The referents of this lexeme in v. 10 are the nations named in v. 11. The referents of the term in v. 15 are a group much larger than the nations on both sides of the Jordan. Therefore, one can apply what the psalmist says about the nations and their idols (vv. 15–18) to the specific nations in v. 10.

The second major connection involves the word מעשה ("work") at the beginning of v. 15b. The root of this noun (עשה) appears in verb form twice in vv. 6–7, which focuses on Yahweh's action. He is able to "make" (עשה) lightning flashes (v. 7) because he "does" (עשה) according to his pleasure (v. 6). In contrast to Yahweh, these idols do not make/do (עשה) anything, but are themselves the "makings" (מעשה) of human hands.[91]

Verse 16 moves the passage from the material and the makers of the idols (v. 15) to their lack of ability to act according to their appearance (vv. 16–17a). The description of their appearance is limited to their heads. The head is the home of four important body parts: eyes, ears, mouth, and nose.[92] Three of these four body parts (eyes, ears, and mouth) are mentioned in vv. 16–17. Although the idols possess these body parts, they are unable to perform their intended function.

The bi-colon of v. 16, which deals with two "head parts" (mouth and eyes), reverses the accent count of v. 15 (4 + 3 → 3 + 4). Semantically, both cola highlight the paradox of the presence of body parts that do not operate as intended. Lexically, every lexeme of the bi-colon has a partner. The two components at the center of each colon (להם and ולא ["to them" and "and not"]) are identical. Both the titles of the body parts (פה ["mouth"] in v. 16a; עינים ["eyes"] in v. 16b) and the verbs (ידברו ["speak"] in v. 16a; יראו ["see"] in v. 16b) are lexically parallel. Internal lexical parallelism occurs between

---

91. McCann, *NIB*, 4:1220; Scoralick, "Hallelujah," 259.

92. Watson (*Classical*, 353–55) discusses "lists of body-parts" in Hebrew poetry.

Poetic Analysis of Psalm 135

the noun and verb in each colon as the verb selected is determined by the normal action of the body part.

Within the present section (vv. 15–18), v. 17 is distinct in two ways. First, it alone differs significantly from the comparable passage in Ps 115.[93] These differences are most prominent in its second colon. Second, in relation to its present context, v.17b breaks the pattern established in the three cola that precede it (vv. 16–17a). These distinctions (discussed below) highlight the importance of v. 17b within this section.

The accent count of this bi-colon continues the pattern of reversal seen in vv. 15 and 16. Its 4 + 3 count is a reversal of the accent count of v. 16 (3 + 4), thus establishing the pattern 4 + 3 → 3 + 4 → 4 + 3 across these three verses. Verse 17a is exactly like v. 16ab in that all the parallels between those two cola also apply to this colon. In addition, the dual body part of this colon (אזנים ["ears"]) parallels the dual body part in v. 16b (עינים ["eyes"]). Unlike v. 16ab, the verb that denotes the action of the body part and the title of the body part itself are both from the same root (אזן) in v. 17a.[94]

If the psalmist had continued quoting Ps 115:4–6 verbatim, v. 17b would have all the same features as the cola of vv. 16–17a and would focus on the fourth "head part," the nose.[95] Instead, the psalmist chose to alter this earlier text and move in a different direction, highlighting the lifelessness of the idols.

The opening particle of this second colon (אף) is prominent for two reasons. First, after reading vv. 16–17a, one expects this fourth colon to be about the fourth "head part," namely, the nose (as in Ps 115:5–6). When one hits אף ("indeed"), his expectations appear to be accurate, at least until he keeps reading. This "semantic trick" leads to a reconsideration of the meaning of אף in the context of this verse.[96] The second reason this particle is prominent is because it is, by its very nature, a marker of emphasis in poetry.[97]

As if the emphasis imparted by אף ("indeed") were not enough, one immediately encounters the very rare expression אין־יש ("there is certainly

---

93. The only change outside of v. 17 is the switch from עצביהם (Ps 115:4) to עצבי הגוים in v. 15.

94. Ps 115:6 uses the verb ישמעו.

95. The second colon of Ps 115:6 reads, אף להם ולא יריחון.

96. Ḥakham (*Psalms 101–150*, 374) identifies this (in relation to Ps 115:6) as "a play on words."

97. BDB (64) notes that it is used "more freq. in poetry, especially as introducing emphatically a new thought." See also Ḥakham, *Psalms 101–150*, 374.

no").⁹⁸ The psalmist could have simply written אין־רוח ("there is no spirit"), but instead he added the superfluous יש ("there is") for emphasis.⁹⁹ Delitzsch draws out this emphasis in his expanded translation of this colon: "also there is not a being of breath, *i.e.* there is no breath at all, not a trace thereof, in their mouth."¹⁰⁰ These idols are completely lifeless!

The last two words of v. 17b inform the reader of what the idols are missing (רוח ["breath"]) and give the location from which it is missing (בפיהם ["in their mouths"]). This answers the "why" of the three preceding colon. Why do the "head parts" of the idols not fulfill their intended purpose? It is because they do not possess a רוח ("breath"), which is the source of life (cf. Ps 104:29).¹⁰¹ Hossfeld and Zenger's comments are particularly perceptive: "because there is no breath in their mouth, they lack what one needs in order to live—and what human beings receive from Yhwh (cf. Gen 2:7; Ps 104:30)."¹⁰² Indeed, man's dependence upon Yahweh for his own רוח ("breath") (Ps 104:29) makes idol worship laughable. Man, who cannot even control the reception of his own רוח ("breath"), certainly cannot give רוח ("breath") to idols, thus highlighting that the idols are simply מעשה ידי אדם ("work of human hands") (v. 15).

The reference to בפיהם ("in their mouths") at the end of v. 17 parallels the first item ("head parts") in each colon of vv. 16–17a. In particular, it is a repetition of the first word in v. 16 (פה ["mouth"]). This repetition of פה on either end of vv. 16–17 coupled with the parallelism of dual body parts in the two middle cola (עינים ["eyes"] [v. 16b] and אזנים ["ears"] [v. 17a]) reveals a chiastic structure within these verses related to the head parts (ab/b'a').¹⁰³

I have already discussed the psalmist's use of an emphatic particle אף and a superfluous word at the beginning of v. 17b. Yet, this is not the only verse in this psalm that has such a pleonasm. Verse 5 also opens with an emphatic particle (כי ["indeed"]) and a superfluous word (אני ["I"]) in order to give prominence to what follows. These parallel emphatic statements

---

98. This expression only appears here and in 1 Sam 21:9.

99. As evidenced by the attempt of the editors of BHS to delete it.

100. Delitzsch, *Commentary*, 326. See Ḥakham, *Psalms 101–150*, 374.

101. Brown (*Seeing the Psalms*, 181) identifies "breath" as "metonymic of earthly life, both human and animal (e.g., 76:12a; 104:29b; 146:4; 150:6), so it distinguishes divinity from idol."

102. Hossfeld and Zenger, *Psalms*, 499.

103. Fokkelman (*Major Poems*, 2:300) also highlights this chiasm and the associated "rhyme with the dual forms used for the senses."

underscore the contrast between these two sections: Yahweh is great, but the idols are dead. McCann has highlighted a second contrast between v. 17 and earlier verses in the psalm. Concerning the twofold repetition of רוח ("wind"/"breath") in this psalm (vv. 7 and 17), he states, "The 'wind' serves God's command, but the idols have no 'wind'—no vital power."[104]

Verse 18—a bi-colon with an accent count of 3 + 3—concludes the psalmist's description of the idols (vv. 15–18). Its opening כ ("like") sets up a comparison between the idols and their builders/worshipers. The second colon builds upon the last word in the first colon (the subject of the verb). As such, it introduces a much broader group (כל אשר־בטח בהם ["all who trust in them"]) that undoubtedly includes the first group (עשיהם ["their makers"]).[105]

Within the present section (vv. 15–18), v. 18 is most closely related to v. 15. One parallel between the two is their positive syntax in contrast to the negative syntax of vv. 16–17 (every colon of these latter verses has a negative particle). The most prominent connection between these two verses is the presence of the root עשה ("do/make") in both of them. In v. 15, מעשה ("work") emphasizes the nature of idols as the products of humans. In v. 18, the focus is on the idol makers (עשיהם ["their makers"]). Another parallel between these two verses is the semantic link between this verse and v. 15a. The phrases עשיהם ("their makers") and כל אשר־בטח בהם ("all who trust in them") in v. 18 parallel הגוים ("the nations") in v. 15a. Thus, the groups of v. 18 are members of the larger group of v. 15.[106]

The major question raised by v. 18 is, In what way are the makers of idols like the idols? Verse 15 obviously does not answer this question since it focuses on the physical material (כסף וזהב ["silver and gold"]) used to make the idols (מעשה ידי אדם ["work of men's hands"]). Verses 16–17, particularly the emphatic statement at the end of v. 17, answer this question. As already noted, vv. 16–17 emphasize the lifeless impotence of the idols. Thus, those who make and trust in them will be lifeless (dead) as well.[107]

---

104. McCann, *NIB*, 4:1220.

105. This may explain the position of the subject (עשיהם) in v. 18a (i.e., it is the last word).

106. Allen (*Psalms 101–150*, 287) notes that the order of these verses (vv. 15–18) "appears to be loosely chiastic" (see also Auffret, "Ton nom pour toujours," 236). These two verses supplement the chiastic structure of vv. 16–17.

107. Goldingay, *Psalms 90–150*, 584–5; Kimḥi, *Commentary*, 67; Augustine, *Expositions*, 531; Alexander, *The Psalms*, 1085.

PART 1: THE POETRY OF PSALMS 135–137

I have already noted the psalmist's use of the root עשׂה ("do/make") in vv. 6, 7, 15, and 18 to highlight the contrast between Yahweh and the idols. An additional phrase in v. 18 further underscores this contrast. The phrase כל אשר only appears in vv. 6 and 18 in this psalm. In v. 6, the Lord does "all which" he desires. In v. 8, "all who" trust in idols become like them. Thus, the Lord's ability to enact all of his desires contrasts with the idols' ability to bring death upon all who trust in them.

Concluding Call to Bless Yahweh (vv. 19–21)

After the desperate picture of the idols and their worshipers in vv. 15–18, the psalmist once again turns his attention to the worship of Yahweh (vv. 19–21). This concluding call to praise is the second half of the inclusio introduced in vv. 1–4. These two stanzas have numerous similarities. The fourfold command of blessing (ברכו) parallels the fourfold command of praise (הללו) in vv. 1–4.[108] A second similarity between the two stanzas is the presence of the direct object marker. It only appears in this psalm in these two section, four times in vv. 19–20 and once in v. 1. Third, both passages mention the group(s) to whom the command is given (i.e., vocative). Fourth, the five appearances of the noun בית ("house") are restricted to these two sections (2 times in vv. 1–3; 3 times in vv. 19–20).

A Call to Bless Yahweh (vv. 19–20)

Within this final stanza (vv. 19–21), vv. 19–20 are the most closely related. These verses give the same command to four different groups. Both bicola have an accent count of 4 + 4 and exhibit parallelism on every level. Lexically and semantically, the verses are almost identical. In fact, the final verbs and direct objects of all four cola are the same (ברכו את־יהוה ["bless Yahweh"]). The only change in each colon is the group mentioned, even though the groups mentioned in the first three cola all begin with the word בית ("house").[109]

Verse 19 contains the first two commands to bless Yahweh, and, consequently, references two of the groups who receive the command. Since

---

108. Hossfeld and Zenger (*Psalms*, 500) write, "Now the psalm uses the (priestly-colored) verb ברך, 'bless' (taking up Pss 115:18; 134:1–2), in order to prepare for the closing blessing" (v. 21).

109. Hence, the first three cola only differ by one word.

the only difference between these two cola is the second word in each, the lone issue in the analysis of this verse is the relationship between these two groups (בית ישׂראל ["house of Israel"] in v. 19a and בית אהרן ["house of Aaron"] in v. 19b). Here there is a move from general to specific. The people as a whole are the referents of בית ישׂראל ("house of Israel") while the priests are the sole referent of בית אהרן ("house of Aaron").

Verse 20a follows the pattern of v. 19ab and only differs from these previous two cola by one word. The group mentioned in this colon is בית הלוי ("house of Levi"). This group served in the temple (as the "house of Aaron" in the previous colon) as temple singers. In fact, this is the only reference to this group in the entire Psalter.[110] Because of their role in the temple, they have more in common with בית אהרן ("house of Aaron") of v. 19b than בית ישׂראל ("house of Israel") in v. 19a.

The reference to יראי יהוה ("Yahweh fearers") in v. 20b breaks the pattern of the initial בית ("house") and expands the possible referents of vv. 19–20. While this term doubtlessly includes members of the first three groups, it can be applied to "all those who take upon themselves God's lordship and service."[111] The use of this broader term in v. 20b reverses the sequence of v. 19. Verse 19 moves from broad to specific whereas v. 20 moves from specific to broad.

One of the key differences between vv. 19–21 and their framing counterpart (vv. 1–4) is the number of addressees. Verses 1–4 mention only one group specifically, but vv. 19–21 designates four groups. However, it appears, based on the numerous links between these two stanzas, that the four groups in vv. 19–20 are simply an expansion of the עבדי יהוה ("servants of Yahweh") of v. 1. In other words, Yahweh's servants are not only those employed in the service of the temple but everyone who fears him both inside and outside of Israel.

Yahweh is Blessed from Zion (v. 21)

The final verse of this psalm is comprised of a bi-colon and a final hallelujah command. The concluding hallelujah completes the hallelujah inclusio

---

110. Terrien, *The Psalms*, 858.

111. Ḥakham (*Psalms 101–150*, 375) lists three possible referents of this phrase: 1) a particular group within Israel, 2) "converts," and 3) "saintly non-Jews." Scoralick ("Hallelujah," 268), Alexander (*The Psalms*, 1086), and Hossfeld and Zenger (*Psalms*, 500) emphasize the inclusion of peoples outside of Israel.

around the psalm. The bi-colon that opens v. 21 begins with the fifth occurrence of the root ברך ("bless") in this final stanza. In contrast to the previous four, the verb in v. 21 is a passive participle stating as a fact what the psalmist commanded in vv. 19–20.

This final bi-colon has an accent count of 3 + 2. The two words of v. 21b are a further description of the subject (יהוה ["Yahweh"]) of v. 21a, identifying the place of his dwelling (ירושלם ["Jerusalem"]). Both cola end with the name of a place, the first designating the place of the worshipers (מציון ["from Zion"])[112] and the second designating the place of Yahweh's dwelling (ירושלם ["Jerusalem"]). These two locations are co-referents in this psalm, thus underscoring Yahweh's presence with his people.[113]

The description of Yahweh dwelling in Jerusalem is yet another link back to vv. 1–4. In these verses, the psalmist mentions the house of Yahweh twice (v. 2). Yahweh's house denotes the place where he dwells and rules over his servants. In addition, Yahweh's house was the place where his servants stood (v. 2). These two facets are reiterated in this final verse where Yahweh and his worshipers are once again in the same place, i.e., Zion/Jerusalem (v. 21).[114]

---

112. Hengstenberg, *Commentary*, 474; Kimḥi, *Commentary*, 67; and Kirkpatrick, *The Book of Psalms*, 776–7. Contra Briggs (*Commentary*, 480–81) and Ḥakham (*Psalms 101–150*, 375), who understand מציון as a reference to the place *of* Yahweh, not the worshipers.

113. Körtig (*Zion*, 139) writes, "A differentiation between Zion and Jerusalem is not present here." (Author's translation of: "Eine Differenzierung zwischen Zion und Jerusalem liegt hier nicht vor.")

114. Alden ("Chiastic Psalms," 207) writes, "The 'house of Yahweh' and 'house of God' of v 2 are of course echoed by 'Zion' and 'Jerusalem' in v 21."

2

Poetic Analysis of Psalm 136

OUTLINE

I. Opening Call to Thanksgiving (vv. 1–3)
    A. Thanksgiving for Yahweh's Goodness (v. 1)
    B. Thanksgiving to the Only God (vv. 2–3)

II. Demonstrations of Yahweh's Uniqueness (vv. 4–25)
    A. Thematic Verse: Yahweh's Uniqueness as Evidenced by his Great Wonders (v. 4)
    B. Yahweh's Uniqueness in His Acts of Creation (vv. 5–9)
        1. Yahweh's Making of the Heavens and the Earth (vv. 5–6)
        2. Yahweh's Making of the Great Lights (vv. 7–9)
    C. Yahweh's Uniqueness in His Historical Works on Israel's Behalf (vv. 10–22)
        1. Yahweh's Deliverance of Israel from Egypt (vv. 10–12)
        2. Yahweh's Division of the Red Sea (vv. 13–15)
        3. Yahweh's Guidance of Israel in the Wilderness (v. 16)
        4. Yahweh's Gift of the Land (v. 17–22)
    D. Yahweh's General Care
        1. Yahweh's Deliverance of Israel (vv. 23–24)
        2. Yahweh's Provision for All Creatures (v. 25)

III. Concluding Call to Thanksgiving (v. 26)

Part 1: The Poetry of Psalms 135–137

POETIC ANALYSIS

The Refrain

The Psalter contains many psalms that include a refrain as part of their structure; however, Psalm 136 stands alone in the Psalter as the only psalm in which a refrain completes each verse. The second colon of each of its twenty-six bi-cola consists of the phrase כי לעולם חסדו ("for his loving-kindness is eternal"),[1] thus giving "a unique compositional and artistic character to the psalm"[2] and casting the entire psalm under the umbrella of Yahweh's loving-kindness.

In his discussion of refrains, Watson suggests that the "distinguishing feature" of a refrain "is its structuring function."[3] For him, this structuring function is exemplified in the psalmists' use of refrains to "segment a poem" into stanzas.[4] While such does not hold true with Ps 136, the refrain certainly plays a pivotal role in the psalm's structure. Primarily, its presence produces symmetry throughout the psalm. Its constant repetition produces a poem that consists only of bi-cola. In addition, its fixed composition contributes to the psalm's accentual rhythm. With the exception of vv. 4, 9, 12, 15, and 24 (the intial cola of the first four verses have an accent count of 4; v. 24a has an accent count of 2), the accent counts of all the initial cola match that of the refrain (accent counts of 3).

In addition, Berlin notes that the refrain of Ps 136 "superimposes similarity (of an extreme type) upon contiguity."[5] In other words, "[t]he psalm preserves its narrative sequence..., but the poetic function has been superimposed on it."[6] Without the refrain, the psalm consists primarily of an historical progression of Yahweh's actions from creation to the defeat of the kings on the east side of the Jordan.[7] While some parallelism is apparent between the first cola of these verses (i.e., vertical parallelism), the presence of the refrain further connects these events by linking each of them

---

1. Raabe (*Psalms Structures*, 167) identifies the refrain of Psalm 136 as an example of a refrain "with a fixed composition."
2. Human, "Psalm 136," 73–74.
3. Watson, *Classical*, 295.
4. Ibid., 297.
5. Berlin, *Dynamics*, 139.
6. Ibid., 138.
7. Goldingay (*Psalms 90–150*, 591) remarks, "[O]ne can imagine that many of the first cola ... would form a natural pair if the psalm did not incorporate the refrain."

with Yahweh's loving-kindness (i.e., horizontal parallelism). Thus, the overt repetition of the refrain produces a commonality between the first cola of the verses.[8]

The refrain also plays an important semantic part in the psalm. The presence of the refrain casts every action described in the first cola in light of Yahweh's eternal loving-kindness.[9] Since the commands for thanksgiving in vv. 1a–3a govern the whole psalm, the initial כי ("for") of the refrain indicates that his eternal loving-kindness is an additional reason for thanksgiving.[10] Furthermore, Goldingay connects the refrain to the theme of Yahweh's superiority, which dominates the psalm.[11] Consequently, the greatest proof of Yahweh's superiority over other gods is his eternal loving-kindness.

Opening Call for Thanksgiving (vv. 1–3)

The opening stanza of Ps 136 consists of three verses, each of which begins with the imperative הודו ("give thanks") followed by a lamed preposition and the object of thanksgiving.[12] With the similar command of v. 26, these verses form an inclusio around the psalm. Moreover, the three imperatives of vv. 1–3 govern each strophe of the psalms's body, as evidenced by the eightfold repetition of the lamed preposition (vv. 4, 5, 6, 7, 10, 13, 16, and 17) and the single occurrence of the relative pronoun ש ("who") (v. 23).

Thanksgiving for Yahweh's Goodness (v. 1)

Verse 1 is identical to Pss 106:1; 107:1; and 118:1, 29. After the opening command of thanksgiving, v. 1a gives the object of thanksgiving (יהוה ["Yahweh"])[13] and a motive clause (כי־טוב ["for he is good"]). This colon is unique in that it contains the only כי ("for") in the psalm that is not part of

---

8. Berlin (*Dynamics*, 139) writes, "The effect then spreads to the first parts of the verses."

9. Barnes, *Notes*, 277.

10. I interpret the כי as introducing a motive clause.

11. Goldingay, *Psalms 90–150*, 597.

12. Hossfeld and Zenger (*Psalms*, 506) highlight the lack of any identification of the addressees of this psalm (in contrast to Ps 135).

13. The mention of Yahweh in this first colon provides the antecedent for the 3ms pronoun at the end of the refrain.

the refrain. Hence, this verse gives two reasons for giving thanks to Yahweh: 1) he is good (v. 1a) and 2) his loving-kindness is eternal (v. 1b).

Lexical parallelism between these two cola is perceptible in the repetition of the lamed preposition and the particle כי ("for") in both cola. In addition, טוב ("good") (v. 1a) and חסד ("loving-kindness") (v. 1b) are a common word pair in the Psalter.[14] They are near synonyms that highlight Yahweh's benevolence. Semantically, this emphasis distinguishes v. 1a and the refrain, which are the only cola that explicitly focus on the attributes of Yahweh rather than his specific actions.[15]

Thanksgiving to the Only God (vv. 2–3)

Verses 2 and 3 focus on the uniqueness of Yahweh, who "has dominion over all beings that are referred to as 'gods.'"[16] These verses exhibit paradigmatic parallelism on both the lexical and semantic levels. Both verses are identical with the exception of different divine names in their second and third lexical positions.[17] As with v. 1, both verses begin with the imperative הודו ("give thanks") followed by a prefixed lamed and a divine appellation. The designation of Yahweh as אלהי האלהים ("God of gods") (v. 2a) and אדני האדנים ("Lord of lords") (v. 3a) comes from Deut 10:17, where Moses uses both phrases to describe Yahweh. The repetition of these phrases in both passages reinforces the point of the passage: Yahweh is above all other gods.

Demonstrations of Yahweh's Uniqueness (vv. 4–25)

The repetition of the lamed preposition without the imperative (הודו ["give thanks"]) upon which it depends signals the transition from the introductory call to the body of the psalm. Thus, beginning in v. 4, four successive lamed prepositions connect back to the threefold introductory call for thanksgiving. Instead of prefacing a divine name (as in vv. 1–3), they are prefixed to substantival participles that describe Yahweh's actions. Perhaps

---

14. Cf. Pss 23:6; 25:7; 63:4; 69:17; 86:5; 100:5; 106:1; 107:1; 109:21; 118:1, 29; and 136:1.

15. The specific acts in the rest of the psalm are examples of his goodness and loving-kindness.

16. Ḥakham, *Psalms 101–150*, 376.

17. The phonological ties are as follows: 1) לאלהי in (v. 2a) and לאדני (v. 3a), and 2) האלהים (v. 2a) and האדנים (v. 3a).

Poetic Analysis of Psalm 136

one of the purposes of this fourfold repetition is to accustom readers of the psalm to read each verse in light of the three imperatives of vv. 1–3 since this construction (lamed preposition plus a participle) becomes less prominent throughout the psalm.

I have divided the body of the psalm into four major stanzas: 1) Thematic Verse: Yahweh's Uniqueness as Evidenced by His Great Wonders (v. 4), 2) Yahweh's Acts of Creation (vv. 5–9), 3) Yahweh's Historical Works on Israel's Behalf (vv. 10–22), and 4) Yahweh's General Care (vv. 23–25).

Thematic Verse: Yahweh's Uniqueness as Evidenced by His Great Wonders (v. 4)

Verse 4 is almost identical to two earlier verses in the Psalter: 72:18 and 86:10. Verse 4a[18] reiterates Yahweh's distinctiveness (as seen in vv. 2–3) by means of the phrase לבדו ("to him alone") at its conclusion. The first part of v. 4a specifies the manner in which he is matchless: his ability to do נפלאות גדלות ("great wonders")[19] (v. 4a) sets him apart as the אלהי האלהים ("God of gods") (v. 2a) and אדני האדנים ("Lord of lords") (v. 3a).[20]

The general nature of this verse's description of Yahweh's works contrasts with the other verses of the body, all of which highlight specific examples of Yahweh's uniqueness. Such a broad quality is apparent in the psalmist's use of the phrase נפלאות גדלות ("great wonders"), which "may mean anything on earth and in heaven Yahweh has accomplished."[21] Hence, this verse stands as the head verse for the section concerning Yahweh's works as Creator (vv. 5–9) *and* the entire body of the psalm (vv. 4–25).[22] Each specific example within the body falls under the umbrella of this broad statement.

---

18. Phonological parallels between v. 4a and the refrain are as follows: 1) לעשׂה (v. 4a) and לעולם (v. 4b), and 2) לבדו (v. 4a) and חסדו (v. 4b) (See Auffret, "Note," 2). These sound repetitions bind the first half of the verse to the refrain.

19. Goldingay (*Psalms 90–150*, 591) states that "escribing them as great wonders might seem redundant . . . [b]ut the adjective underlines their significance."

20. Hossfeld and Zenger (*Psalms*, 506) write, "This [wonders] is a summary term for Yhwh's creating and liberating/redeeming actions."

21. Gerstenberger, *Psalms*, 386.

22. Cf. McCann, *NIB*, 4:1224; Scoralick, "Hallelujah," 261; Mays, *Psalms*, 419.

PART 1: THE POETRY OF PSALMS 135–137

Yahweh's Uniqueness in His Acts of Creation (vv. 5–9)

The dominant structural feature of this stanza (vv. 5–9) is the repetition of the lamed preposition plus a substantive participle at the beginning of each of the first three verses.[23] This stanza consists of two strophes: 1) vv. 5–6 describe Yahweh's making of the heavens and the earth and 2) vv. 7–9 recount his making of the great lights. As with v. 4, לעשה ("to him who made") (vv. 5 and 7) appears at the beginning of each strophe.

YAHWEH'S MAKING OF THE HEAVENS AND THE EARTH (VV. 5–6)

The first specific examples of Yahweh's "great wonders" are found in vv. 5–6: Yahweh's making of the heavens and the earth. Verse 5 opens with a repetition of the initial phrase of v. 4 (לעשה ["to him who made"]). Whereas v. 4a has a timeless connotation, this colon refers to specific acts of Yahweh in the past, i.e., his wise making of the heavens.[24]

Verse 6a continues the pattern of the initial lamed plus a participle. However, the psalmist does not use the verb עשה ("made"), but the less common רקע ("stamped") to describe Yahweh's action. This verb, in conjunction with the concluding prepositional phrase of the colon (על־המים ["upon the waters"]), parallels passages such as Exod 20:4 and Ps 24:2, which portray the land as "a covering stretched out over the water that is below the earth."[25]

The parallels between vv. 5a and 6a are extensive. On the lexical level, the qal participles follow the typical pattern of moving from a general term to a more poetic term (עשה ["made"] is prevalent in the creation account of Gen 1–2 [e.g., 1:7, 16, 25, 26; 2:2–4] while רקע ["stamped"] appears exclusively in poetic texts when referring to creation [e.g. Isa 42:5; 44:24]). In addition, the terms differ in their placement on the literal/figurative continuum. The first verb (עשה) is literal, but the second (רקע) is a figurative verb that draws on the imagery of a goldsmith who beats out metal plating.[26]

23. When viewed in light of v. 4, there are four consecutive verses that begin in this manner.

24. Cf. Jer 10:12; 51:15; and Prov 3:19. Ḥakham (*Psalms 101–150*, 376) discusses two ways of reading בתבונה.

25. Ibid., 377.

26. Examples of the literal use of this verb include Exod 39:3; Num 17:4; Isa 40:19; and Jer 10:9.

Poetic Analysis of Psalm 136

Thus, the move from v. 5a to v. 6a is both from broad to particular and from literal to figurative.

A second word pair is the common הארץ/השמים ("the heavens"/"the earth"). The use of these words to describe the two spheres (i.e., merism) of God's creative work is common in Gen 1–2 (1:1; 2:1, 3, 4).[27] Closely related to these two realms is the third sphere of creation (המים ["the waters"]), which appears in the prepositional phrase that concludes v. 6a.[28] Thus, like Ps 135:6, there is a move from the higher to lower parts of creation in these two verses (המים ← הארץ ← השמים).

The relationship between the two prepositional phrases that conclude the cola of vv. 5a and 6a is syntagmatic. Both are adverbial prepositional phrases, but each answers a different question. The concluding phrase of v. 5a (בתבונה ["in wisdom"]) tells how Yahweh made the heavens. The prepositional phrase of v. 6a (על־המים ["upon the waters"]), on the other hand, tells where Yahweh performed his beating out of the earth.

Yahweh's Making of the Great Lights (vv. 7–9)

After the big picture description of God's act of creation in vv. 5–6, the vv. 7a–9a focus on God's work on the fourth day of creation, i.e., his making of the great lights.[29] The vocabulary and syntax of this strophe is very similar to that of Gen 1:16.

Verse 7, like vv. 4 and 5, begins with לעשה ("to him who made"), marking the third and last verse to begin this way. Each time this phrase begins a verse, the object of Yahweh's making gets more specific, moving from his *doing* "great wonders" (v. 4a) to his *making* of "the heavens" (v. 5a) to his *making* of "the great lights" (v. 7a).

Verse 7a's connections with vv. 4a and 5a go beyond the lexical, grammatical, and phonological parallels associated with this opening phrase.[30] First, this verse parallels v. 5a on the semantic level since both verses high-

---

27. Berlin (*Dynamics*, 76) classifies these terms as "conventionalized coordinates." Hossfeld and Zenger (*Psalms*, 507) also connect the phrase כי־טוב of v. 1 with the same phrase in Genesis 1 (6x).

28. המים (v. 6a) also rhymes with השמים (v. 5a).

29. Hossfeld and Zenger (*Psalms*, 507) write, "vv. 4–6 refer to the creation of . . . a cosmic structure . . . , while vv. 7–9 describes [sic] the equipment of this structure."

30. The repetition of לעשה (v. 7a) continues the ע-ל combination that has been so prevalent in this psalm. There is also rhyme across vv. 5a–7a (השמים in v. 5a; המים in v. 6a; אורים גדלים in v. 7a).

light some aspect of Yahweh's creative work as recorded in Gen 1. In fact, if read in light of Gen 1, v. 5a describes Yahweh's preparation of a home for the "great lights" of v. 7a. Second, it parallels v. 4a on the lexical level, with the first (לעשׂה ["to him who does/made"]) and last (גדל ["great"]) words of v. 7a echoing v. 4a. The repetition of גדל ("great") indicates that the "great lights" are one example of the "great wonders" of Yahweh.

The pattern of verses opening with a lamed preposition prefixed to a qal participle ceases with vv. 8–9. These verses both begin with the poetically rare direct object marker.[31] In both instances, it is a signal of apposition. The mention of the "great lights" in v. 7a leads to an identification of these lights and the time of their respective dominions in vv. 8a–9a.

These verses exhibit almost perfect parallelism on the grammatical, lexical, and semantic levels, the only peculiarity being the presence of וכוכבים ("and stars") in v. 9a.[32] On the lexical level, the repetition of the noun ממשלה ("dominion") in the middle of both verses underscores the focus of these verses, namely, the dominion of the great lights.[33] In both verses, the name of the lights precedes this noun and the designation of the time of their dominion follows it. The first lexical pairing involves the day light (השמשׁ ["the sun"]) (v. 8a) and the two night-lights (הירח וכוכבים ["the moon and stars"]) (v. 9a). This contrast between the names of the lights corresponds to the contrast between the times of their dominion given at the end of each colon (יום ["day"] in v. 8a; לילה ["night"] in v. 9a). The word pair לילה/יום ("day"/"night") extends back to the first day of creation where God separated the light from the darkness (Gen 1:3–5). Just as vv. 5a–6a highlighted the two major realms of creation, so vv. 8a–9a focus on the two major times of creation and their corresponding governing light(s). Thus, the maker of the great lights (v. 7a) is the one who determines their dominion (vv. 8a–9a).

---

31. The two direct object markers in vv. 8–9 are the only appearances of this particle in this psalm.

32. The reason I label this a peculiarity is because of the difference between this text and Gen 1:16, which does not mention the dominion of the stars.

33. The repetition of ממשלה in both verses produces two phonological parallels: 1) שמשׁ (v. 8a), ממשלת (v. 8a), and ממשלות (v. 9a); and 2) לממשלת (v. 8a), לממשלות (v. 9a), and לעולם (refrain).

Poetic Analysis of Psalm 136

Yahweh's Uniqueness in His Historical Works on Israel's Behalf (vv. 10–22)

After describing Yahweh's creation of the heavens, earth, and great lights, the psalmist turns his attention in vv. 10a–22a to Yahweh's historical works on behalf of his people. This stanza consists of four strophes, each highlighting a different act of Yahweh. Each new strophe begins with a lamed preposition plus a qal participle.[34] The four strophes are as follows: 1) Yahweh's Deliverance of Israel from Egypt (vv. 10–12), 2) Yahweh's Division of the Red Sea (vv. 13–15), 3) Yahweh's Guidance of Israel in he Wilderness (v. 16), and 4) Yahweh's Defeat of the Kings on the East of the Jordan (vv. 17–22).[35]

Yahweh's Deliverance of Israel from Egypt (vv. 10–12)

The pattern of verses beginning with a lamed preposition plus a qal participle, which is absent from vv. 8–9, reappears in v. 10.[36] The lamed preposition once again orients the reader's focus toward the threefold הודו ("give thanks") of vv. 1a–3a. Yahweh's deliverance of Israel from Egypt is yet another reason for thanksgiving (vv. 10a–12a).

Verse 10a recounts the last Egyptian plague—the striking of the firstborn—using the standard verb (נכה ["strike"]) associated with this event.[37] This final plague served as the impetus behind Pharaoh's willingness to release the people of Israel.[38] The unique syntax of this verse places the emphasis on מצרים ("Egypt") instead of בכור ("firstborn").[39] Ḥakham explains this emphasis well when he writes, "The psalmist means that although only

---

34. For support on the isolation of v. 16, see Watson, *Classical*, 176.

35. Goldingay (*Psalms 90–150*, 592) highlights the omission of the patriarchs and Sinai in this stanza.

36. Two phonological parallels bind the two major stanzas of this psalm together: 1) לממשלת (v. 8a), לממשלות (v. 9a), and למכה (v. 10a); and 2) וכוכבים (v. 9a) and בבכוריהם (v. 10a).

37. Goldingay (*Psalms 90–150*, 592) cites the Torah texts of Exod 12:12, 13, 29, and Anderson (*Psalms 73–150*, 895) cites Pss 78:51 and 135: 8 as examples.

38. Briggs (*Commentary*, 483) notes that the psalmist uses "the supreme plague as a specimen."

39. בכור במצרים (or בכורי מצרים) is the object of Yahweh's striking in Pss 78:51; 105:36; and 135:8.

the firstborn actually died, the plague was a severe blow to all Egypt."[40] In other words, this verse stresses God's judgment on all of the Egyptians, not just a part thereof.

Verse 11a continues the story of the Pentateuch by describing the Lord's deliverance of Israel from Egypt and contains the first reference to Israel in this psalm. Yahweh's favorable actions toward Israel (v. 11a) contrast with his destructive actions against the Egyptians (v. 10a). Like v. 10a, the language used by the psalmist is the standard language used in the Pentateuchal narration of this event.[41]

The use of the wayyiqtol at the beginning of v. 11 serves as a notice that this verse is a continuation of v. 10a.[42] Yet, this is not the only thing that connects these two verses.[43] The referents of the two proper nouns (מצרים ["Egypt"] in v. 10a; ישראל ["Israel"] in v. 11a) contrast one another. This contrast may have been one of the reasons for the syntax of v. 10a. By placing מצרים ("Egypt") as the object of the verb in v. 10a, the psalmist sets up a contrast between the Egyptians and Israel, and in particular, Yahweh's actions toward each nation.

The focus on Yahweh's deliverance of his people from Egypt (v. 11a) leads to an anthropomorphic description of Yahweh's demonstration of his power in carrying out this great work (v. 12a).[44] The two prepositional phrases of v. 12a are common in the Pentateuch's description of this same event.[45] Augustine refers to these two expressions as "favourite Mosaic figures for the active and energetic exercise of power."[46] The image reflected in these "figures" is that of a "human warrior" who exhibits great strength and stands ready to smite his enemies.[47]

Since v.12a divides into two parts, it exhibits internal parallelism. Both halves have the same surface structure (preposition-noun-adjective) and

---

40. Ḥakham, *Psalms 101–150*, 377.

41. Goldingay (*Psalms 90–150*, 592) notes that v. 11a is most like Exod 7:5.

42. Ḥakham, *Psalms 101–150*, 378.

43. Hossfeld and Zenger (*Psalms*, 507) identify a "subtle worldplay" between למכה (v. 10a) and מתוכם (v. 11a).

44. Verse 12—with its accent count of 4 + 3—breaks this psalm's normal accent pattern of 3 + 3. The last verse with this same accent count was v. 9. Both are the final verses in their respective strophes.

45. Augustine (*Expositions*, 532) cites Exod 6:1, 6; 13:9; 14:12; Deut 4:34; 5:15; 7:19; 11:2; 26:8.

46. Ibid.

47. Ḥakham, *Psalms 101–150*, 378.

emphasize the great power of Yahweh. On the lexical level, both phrases are examples of what Berlin called "conventionalized coordinates."[48]

The prepositional phrases of v. 12a also resonate with a few previous verses. First, they complement the prepositional phrases at the end of vv. 10a–11a. The prepositional phrase of v. 10a answers the "who" question, that of v. 11a answers the "where" question, and the two prepositional phrases of v.12a answer the "how" question. They also parallel the similar prepositional phrase in v. 5a. Both of these ב ("with") prepositional phrases are adverbial phrases that describe the manner by which Yahweh carried out his action. Verse 5a emphasizes his wisdom in creation, and v. 12a emphasizes his might in bringing his people out of Israel.

Yahweh's Division of the Red Sea (vv. 13–15)

This strophe picks up where the previous strophe ended. After Yahweh's deliverance of Israel from Egypt, one obstacle remained: the Red Sea. These verses recount Yahweh's division of the Red Sea, an act that resulted in the salvation of his people and the death of Pharaoh and his troops.

The structure of vv. 13a–15a is nearly identical to that of the previous strophe (vv. 10–12). It begins with a lamed preposition prefixed to a qal participle and its concluding verse has an accent count of 4 + 3. One difference between the two sections is the presence of a verb in each of the verses in vv. 13a–15a. Moreover, the references to the Red Sea at the beginning of v. 13a and the end of v. 15a form a frame around the strophe.[49]

Verse 13a describes Yahweh's division of the Red Sea with unique language.[50] Because the initial participle and the concluding noun are both from the same root, this colon exhibits significant consonance. The first six consonants of the verse (לגזר ים ["to him who divided the sea"]) reappear as the last six consonants in the prepositional phrase לגזרים ("to parts"). The only consonants not repeated in this verse are those in the word סוף ("Red").[51]

---

48. Berlin, *Dynamics*, 76.

49. Hossfeld and Zenger, *Psalms*, 507; Ḥakham, *Psalms 101–150*, 378. Auffret ("Note," 4) identifies a word play between the phrase בים־סוף (vv. 13–15a) and ביד (v. 12a).

50. The verb גזר only appears here in reference to this historical event (Allen, *Psalms 101–150*, 297–8). Furthermore, the object of the preposition in v. 13a (גזרים) only appears twice in the Hebrew Bible (here and Gen 15:17).

51. Additionally, לגזר and לגזרים resonate with ובזרוע (v.12a), binding the two strophes

Part 1: The Poetry of Psalms 135–137

The mention of a sea (ים) in v. 13a echoes the mention of the waters (המים) in v. 6a. Auffret connects Yahweh's lordship over the waters at creation (v. 6a) to his division of the Red Sea during the Exodus (v. 13a).[52] In v. 6a Yahweh's work took place *on* (על) the waters, but in vv. 13a–15a the realm of Yahweh's work is *in* (בתוכו in v. 14a and ב in v. 15a) the sea.

Verse 14a continues the progression of events by describing Yahweh leading Israel through the Red Sea and has strong ties to v. 11a. Interestingly enough, vv. 11a and 14a are the center verses in their respective strophes. As such, both highlight God's "moving" of Israel. In v. 11a he brings them out of Egypt In v. 14a, he takes them through the Red Sea. The psalmist reinforces the movement of these verses by using hiphil verbs (ויוצא ["and he brought out"] in v. 11a; והעביר ["and he caused to pass"] in v. 14a) and repeating ישראל ("Israel") and תוך ("in the midst of") in both verses.[53] Yahweh's moving of Israel in vv. 10a–22a does not stop in v. 14a, but as will become evident, continues to the lands of Sihon and Og (vv. 21a–22a).

The narration of Yahweh's work at the Red Sea concludes in v. 15a with a description of Yahweh's destruction of Pharaoh and his army. As in v. 14a, the language of this verse echoes the record of this event in Exod 14. In fact, these are the only two passages where the verb נער ["shook out"] describes Yahweh's destruction of the Egyptians in the Red Sea.[54]

Verse 15a contrasts with v. 14a. Yahweh's work with Israel was deliverance (v. 14a), but Yahweh's work against Pharaoh and his army was judgment (v. 15a). This is not the first time Israel and Egypt have stood in contrast. The previous strophe (vv. 10–12) began with Yahweh's judgment of the Egyptians and then moved to Yahweh's deliverance of Israel. In this strophe (vv. 13–15), the order is reversed. Yahweh's judgment of Pharaoh and his army (v. 15a) follows Israel's rescue (v. 14a). Therefore, these two contrasts serve as a frame around these two sections.

Yahweh's Guidance of Israel in the Wilderness (v. 16)

Verse 16a concisely summarizes God's care for Israel during their time in the wilderness. The language of v. 16a echoes the description of this same

---

together at the seam.

52. Auffret, "Note," 10.

53. Hossfeld and Zenger (*Psalms*, 507) highlight the significance of תוך in both verses.

54. Typically, the verb נער refers to the shaking out of a garment. Just as a man shakes out his garment, so also the Lord shook out Pharaoh and his army into the Red Sea.

Poetic Analysis of Psalm 136

period in Israel's past found in Deut 8:15. Unlike the other strophes in this stanza, this strophe consists of only this single verse.[55] The presence of the lamed preposition and the participle at the beginning of this verse signals the possibility of a new section.[56] The subject matter of this verse confirms that the psalmist has indeed begun a new strophe.[57] He switches from Yahweh's deliverance of his people at the Red Sea to his care for them in the wilderness.

Scoralick mentions two other features that distinguish this verse from the other portions of the historical review (vv. 10a–22a).[58] First, there is no mention of God's actions against another power (Egypt in vv. 10a–12a, the Red Sea in vv. 13a–15a, and kings in vv. 17a–22a). Second, of the four strophes within vv. 10a–22a, only this one does not specifically mention Israel. Instead, v. 16a uses the term עמו ("his people"), marking the only instance of this lexeme in this psalm.

This verse continues the focus of vv. 10a–15a on God's "moving" of Israel. He brought them out of Egypt (v. 11a), through the Red Sea (v. 14a), and now through the wilderness (v. 16a). The surface structure of v. 16a is the same as that of many of the previous verses in this larger section (verb-object-prepositional phrase). In particular, it has strong connections with vv. 11a and 14a, both of which focus on Yahweh's moving of Israel. The verbs and objects of all three verses exhibit paradigmatic parallelism. All three verbs are "going" verbs that appear in the hiphil whose objects denote Israel. The only difference between these three verses is the different places mentioned in the prepositional phrases at the end of each verse.

When it comes to phonological correspondences, v. 16a participates in an important group of consonant clusters on the level of the stanza. The מ-ל-כ grouping (למוליך ["to him who led"]) echoes למכה ("to him who struck") in v. 10a, and as will become evident, strikes a cord that resonates into the next strophe. The repetition of this cluster of constantants at key points throughout vv. 10–18 serves to reinfornce the constant care of Yahweh from the beginning (v. 10) to the end of Israel's journey (vv. 17–18).

---

55. Along with vv. 25 and 26, Watson (*Classical*, 172) identifies v. 16 as a monocolon combined with a refrain. Cf. Auffret, "Note," 5; and Mays, *Psalms*, 419

56. Although not every instance of this construction in the psalm marks a new strophe (cf. vv. 6–7), it has initiated every new strophe up to this point, and within this stanza (vv. 10–22), every occurrence of this construction marks a new strophe. See also Auffret, "Note," 5.

57. Rensburg, "History as Poetry," 86, identifies v. 16 as a "transition."

58. Scoralick, "Hallelujah," 266.

Part 1: The Poetry of Psalms 135–137

Yahweh's Gift of the Land (vv. 17–22)

The psalmist's rehearsal of Yahweh's great historical works concludes with a lengthy description of his defeat of the kings on the east side of the Jordan and his giving of their land to Israel as an inheritance. Once again, a lamed preposition followed by a participle (v. 17a) marks the beginning of this strophe. Just like the strophe on the Exodus (vv. 10a–12a), the first verse of this section begins with למכה ("to him who struck") and the second verse begins with a wayyiqtol verb.

This strophe divides into two subsections: 1) vv. 17–20 and 2) vv. 21–22. The first subsection is about Yahweh's defeat of mighty kings and the second concerns his gift of their land to Israel. The prominent feature in the first subsection (vv. 17a–20a) is the repetition of the root מלך ("king") as the middle word in each of these four cola. Not only does this repetition bind these four verses together but it also connects this section with v. 16a, whose opening participle (למוליך) has the same consonantal sequence.[59]

The description of Yahweh's victory over great and mighty kings (vv. 17a–20a) further divides into two parts: 1) vv. 17a–18a and 2) vv. 19a–20a. The first two verses (vv. 17a–18a) tell of Yahweh's destruction of great and mighty kings without specifically naming any of these kings. These verses are identical on almost every level. The lexical parallelism revolves around the repetition of מלכים ("kings") in the second slot of each verse. The verbs (נכה ["strike"] in v. 17a; הרג ["kill"] in v. 18a) and the adjectives (גדלים ["great"] in v. 17a; אדירים ["majestic"] in v. 18a) at each end of these verses parallel each other as near synonyms.[60]

The phonological parallels between these two verses go beyond the repetition of מלכים in both verses. The מ-ל-כ combination is also present in the first word of v. 17a (למכה). Thus, the first two words of v. 17a resonate phonologically with each other and with the first word of v. 16a.[61]

---

59. Ibid. Goldingay (*Psalms 90–150*, 594) writes, "Yhwh is 'taking' them (*môlîk*), an activity than involves putting a great and majestic king (*melek*) such as Sihon or Og in his place."

60. Kimḥi (*Commentary*, 75) notes the synonymy of these verbs.

61. Fokkelman, *Major Poems*, 3:309. He writes, "the play on MLK ... is so extensive that three different conjugations are being juggled around ... Because of the preposition and the participle, *hlk in v. 16a and *nkh (both Hiphil) in v. 17a now co-operate with the fourfold root *mlk*. Note that *lᵉmakkeh* here precedes 'the king(s)' (the regular *mlk*) and how the different order of the three consonants already suggests that the kings will be brought down."

Poetic Analysis of Psalm 136

The parallelism between these verses and earlier portions of this psalm revolve around the first and last words of v. 17a. The opening lamed plus participle of v. 17a (למכה ["to him who struck"]) is identical to that of v. 10a.[62] This is significant because it shows that Israel's journey from Egypt (v. 10a–12a) to the lands of Og and Sihon (vv. 17a–22a) began and ended in the same way, i.e., by Yahweh striking (נכה) their enemies. In the first instance, his striking was to bring his people out (v. 11a) while in the second instance, his purpose was to give his people the land (vv. 21a–22a).[63]

In addition, the last word of v. 17a (גדלים ["great"]) is a repetition of the adjective used in v. 4a to describe Yahweh's wonders (גדלות ["great"]). Since v. 4a sets the tone for the whole body of the psalm (i.e., Yahweh's great wonders distinguish him from other gods), v. 17a serves as one example of Yahweh's great wonders and demonstrates that Yahweh's greatness is greater than the greatness of the kings he destroys.

The focus on the kings Yahweh slaughtered continues in vv. 19a–20a with the identification of the two east-Jordanian kings whom God gave into the hands of Israel, i.e., Og and Sihon. These two kings are specific examples of the מלכים גדלים ("great kings") and מלכים אדירים ("majestic kings") of vv. 17a–18a. Consequently, vv. 19a–20a stand in apposition to the objects of vv. 17a–18a. Unlike the other lamed prepositions that begin verses in this psalm, the lamed prepositions at the beginning of these two verses function as direct object markers.[64] Therefore, the verbs of vv. 17a–18a govern these two cola (vv. 19a–20a).

The parallelism between vv. 19a and 20a extends to almost every level. Grammatically, the verses are identical. In addition to the repetition of מלך ("king"), these verses contain two other word pairs: 1) the names of the kings (סיחון ["Sihon"] in v. 17a; עוג ["Og"] in v. 18a) and 2) the names of their respective kingdoms (האמרי ["the Amorites"] in v. 17a; הבשן ["Bashan"] in v. 18a).

---

62. Goldingay (*Psalms 90–150*, 594) points out that the Torah does not use "hitting or slaying language" to describe the victories over these kings.

63. Fokkelman (*Major Poems*, 3:308–9) writes concerning this "network of *mlk*-verses": "a net in which hostile kings are caught and eliminated."

64. Fokkelman (*Major Poems*, 3:308) highlights the "surprise" associated with these two lamed prepositions: "In . . . vv. 19–20 . . . ,the poet springs a surprise on us. All of a sudden the preposition is used to the detriment of two enemies, the result of now being connected as *nota obiecti* to *hrg* in v. 18, a verb that even does double duty across a strophe boundary."

Verses 21a–22a complete the description of Yahweh's triumph over great kings by highlighting his benevolent action toward his people, i.e., giving them the land of the great kings. Based on these final two verses, this strophe (vv. 17–22) is similar to the first two strophes within vv. 10–22. In vv. 10a–12a, 13a–15a, and here (vv. 17a–22a), the psalmist describes both Yahweh's actions against other nations or powers and his munificent actions toward his people Israel.

The parallelism between these two verses is clearly syntagmatic since v. 22a completes the thought of v. 21a. The repetition of נחלה ("inheritance") at the end of v. 21a and at the beginning of v. 22a is the lexical knot that binds these verses together. This anadiplosis focuses these verses on the purpose for Yahweh gift of the land to Israel: he gave it to them as a possession.[65]

The verb that opens v. 21a (נתן ["gave"]) governs both verses. Its direct object is in v. 21a (ארצם ["their land"]) and its indirect object is in v. 22a (לישראל ["to Israel"]). The use of this verb in reference to Yahweh's favorable action toward Israel distinguishes it from the other verbs within vv. 10a–22a, which focus on Yahweh's actions on behalf of Israel. As noted earlier, the other verbs (vv. 11a, 14a, and 16a) are "moving" verbs (as evidenced by the hiphil stem) that portray Yahweh as the guide for his people. This verb, on the other hand, focuses on Yahweh as the one who gives to his people.

The presence of the 3mp-suffixed pronoun on the direct object links these verses with vv. 17a–20a since the kings of these verses serve as the antecedents of this pronoun. This pronoun also heightens the contrast between vv. 21a and 22a. The land that Yahweh gave was not just any land; it was the land that belonged to great and mighty kings. As a component of the second word of v. 21a, this pronoun contrasts with the second word of v. 22a: Israel. The land that the kings had *possessed* became the *possession* of Israel. The land no longer belonged to the mighty kings, but to the people who belonged to the אלהי האלהים ("God of gods") and אדני האדנים ("Lord of lords") (v. 2a–3a).

The mention of ארצם ("their land") also links these verses to the initial strophe of the body of the psalm (vv. 5a–6a).[66] In v. 6a, the psalmist de-

---

65. Goldingay (*Psalms 90–150*, 595) writes concerning this repetition: "[T]he repetition of a 'possession' before the continuance of v. 22 emphasizes the significance of this notion: *those people's* land became a *possession* for Israel!"

66. Fokkelman (*Major Poems*, 3:310) writes, "The word *'ereṣ* appears twice in this poem, both times exactly placed in the sixth position from the edges (vv. 6 and v. 21) [sic]."

scribes Yahweh as רקע הארץ על־המים ("he who stamped the earth upon the waters"). As the maker of the ארץ ("earth/land") (v. 6a), he alone enjoys the right to apportion it to whomever he chooses.[67] In vv. 21a–22a, he demonstrates his ability to do just that. The land of the great kings ultimately was his land and thus his to give to his people.

The reference to Israel as עבדו ("his servant") in v. 22a is exceptional in this psalm.[68] In every strophe within vv. 10–22, the psalmist references them by their name ישראל ("Israel") (vv. 11a and 14a) or as עמו ("his people") (v. 16a). Here, he identifies them by their name and then adds עבדו ("his servant") appositionally. This additional modifier clarifies the reason for Yahweh's preferential treatment of Israel over the mighty kings. As Israel's Lord, he provides a possession/inheritance for his servant.

This description of Israel as עבדו ("his servant") also parallels v. 16a, where the psalmist describes Yahweh leading עמו ("his people") in the wilderness. These two designations emphasize the people's close relationship to Yahweh as opposed to the more neutral designation ישראל ("Israel") (vv. 11a & 14a).

The final word of v. 22a (עבדו) ["his servant"]) resonates with לבדו ("to him alone") in v. 4a. This connection serves two functions. First, it highlights Yahweh's gift of the land to Israel as one way he demonstrates that he alone is capable of doing great wonders. Second, it creates an inclusion around vv. 4a–22a, which is appropriate since the description of Yahweh's works is more general in vv. 23a–24a than the description of his specific acts in vv. 5a–22a.

Yahweh's General Care (vv. 23–25)

The final stanza (vv. 23–25) of the body is distinct from the other stanzas in many ways. First, vv. 23a–24a are the only verses in the psalm that are in the first person plural (the 1cp pronominal suffix occurs four times in these verses).[69] Second, the relative pronoun שׁ ("who"), which begins v.

---

67. Allen, *Psalms 101–150*, 298.

68. This use of the singular in reference to Israel as a whole is also exceptional, appearing only in Isaiah and Jeremiah. Allen (*Psalms 101–150*, 298) lists Isa 41:8, 9; 44:1, 2. Goldingay (*Psalms 90–150*, 595) names Jer 30:10; 46:27–28.

69. Allen (*Psalms 101–150*, 298) comments on the significance of the first person plural perspective: "The exodus is reviewed, now as God's act of faithful deliverance, not merely of a generation dead and gone but of 'us.'"

23a, appears only here in the psalm. Indeed, its appearance in v. 23a breaks the psalm's dominant pattern of beginning each new section with a lamed preposition and a qal participle. Closely related to the pattern of lamed plus qal participle is the position of the verb in v. 23a. Up to this point in the psalm, the verb or substantive participle has been in the initial position of every verse that contains a verb or participle. In contrast, a prepositional phrase occupies the first position of v. 23a while the participle is in the second position. A fourth difference in this final section is the occurrence of the "only plain perfect tense in our psalm [זכר] (v. 23a)."[70] Fifth, v. 25a opens with the only "unprefixed participle"[71] in the psalm. The last difference between vv. 23a–25a and the other stanzas within the body is thematic. From v. 5a through v. 22a, every verse relates to a specific historical event. However, vv. 23a–25a have a far more general flare than these other verses.

The sole stylistic similarity between this final stanza and the other stanzas is the wayyiqtol in the head position of v. 24a. This is the third example of this pattern in this psalm (the wayyiqtol also appears in vv. 11a and 18a). In each case, the wayyiqtol ensures that the reader will interpret the second verse of the strophe as a continuation of the preceding verse.

This section divides into two strophes: 1) vv. 23–24 and 2) v. 25. A couple of features distinguish these two strophes.[72] First, the 1cp perspective of vv. 23a–24a contrasts with the third person perspective of v. 25a. Second, there is a contrast between Yahweh's dealing with his people (vv. 23a–24a) and all flesh (v. 25a). This move from salvation (his people) to creation (all flesh) in these two strophes reverses the move from creation (vv. 5a–9a) to salvation (vv. 10a–22a) in vv. 5a–22a.[73]

Yahweh's Deliverance of Israel (vv. 23–24)

Verses 23a–24a highlight Yahweh's deliverance of his people from their enemies. Although they have different accent counts, their letter count is identical (both have 13 letters).[74] The parallels between these two cola are

---

70. Gerstenberger, *Psalms*, 387.

71. Ibid.

72. Brennan ("Hidden Harmonies," 142) states that "[t]he entire composition [of Psalm 136] pivots around verses 23–24, though translations rarely convey this."

73. Mays, *Psalms*, 420; Auffret, "Note," 10.

74. Verse 23a has an accent count of three. Verse 24a is the only colon with an accent count of two.

strongest on the grammatical and phonological levels.⁷⁵ On the lexical and semantic levels, the parallelism is syntagmatic. Verse 24a is continues the thought of v. 23a by clarifying the exact nature of both Israel's lowliness and Yahweh's remembrance. The psalmist clarifies Israel's lowliness in v. 24a as "enemy oppression."⁷⁶ Moreover, the visible evidence of Yahweh's remembrance of his people is his deliverance of them from their enemies.⁷⁷ The semantic parallelism is therefore consequential. Verse 24a describes the consequences of Yahweh's remembering (v. 23a), viz., his deliverance of his people from their enemies.

When compared to vv. 10a–22a, vv. 23a–24a are distinct in that they do not mention a specific historical event (as did each strophe within vv. 10a–22a). Thus, one of the key interpretive issues surrounding these verses is the exact historical event(s) to which they refer. Hossfeld and Zenger aptly describe the number of opinions regarding this issue when they observe, "The spectrum of opinions is very broad."⁷⁸ Their own solution is not to connect it to any specific historical event, but as "the dramatic history of Israel since the beginnings narrated in vv. 10–22."⁷⁹ This textual interpretation is far more attractive than many of the historical interpretations offered.⁸⁰

Some commentators identify a word play between מצרינו ("from our enemies") (v. 24) and מצרים ("Egypt") (v. 10).⁸¹ The locations of these two words areis significant, viz., they appear in the first and last verses of a larger section dealing with Yahweh's works on behalf of Israel (vv. 10–24). Thus, references to his deliverance of Israel from their enemies frame Ps 136's focus on Yahweh's acts for his people. This phonological parallel is further supported by the semantic similarity between the verbs of vv. 11a

---

75. The phonological parallelism revolves around the repetition of נו at the end of the first and last words of each colon. Additionally, both cola have internal phonological parallels: 1) שבשפלנו and לנו (v. 23a); and 2) ויפרקנו and מצרינו (v. 24a).

76. Allen, *Psalms 101–150*, 299.

77. The verb of v. 24 (פרק) refers to the snatching or dragging away of something. See BDB, 830 and HALOT 3:975.

78. Hossfeld and Zenger, *Psalms*, 508.

79. Ibid. Rensburg ("History as Poetry," 86) notes that these verses "are in the form of an epilogue where author and audience identify themselves (He remembered us . . . and rescued us . . .) with Israel of long ago." Cf. Auffret, "Note," 8.

80. See Goldingay (*Psalms 90–150*, 595–96) for a discussion of the following options: 1) the period of the Judges, 2) the exile, and 3) after the exile.

81. Fokkelman, *Major Poems*, 3:310; Allen, *Psalms 101–150*, 299.

(יצא) and 24a (פרק). Just as he "brought out" Israel from Egypt (v. 11a), so he also "snatched" them from their enemies (v. 24a), one of which was the Egyptians.

Yahweh's Provision for All Creatures (v. 25)

As previously mentioned, the unprefixed qal participle of v. 25a is unique in this psalm. In some sense, this form not only separates this verse from vv. 23a–24a, but also separates this verse from all the verses in the psalm. The universal scope of this verse confirms this separation. In contrast to vv. 10a–24a, which stress Yahweh's works for Israel, v. 25a draws attention to Yahweh's care for all creatures using language common to other psalms (Pss 104:27–30; 145:15ff.) and the Genesis account of Yahweh's creative activity (see Gen 1:29–30).[82]

Within the psalm, this universal perspective parallels the description of Yahweh's making of the heavens and the earth in vv. 5a–9a.[83] These two passages form an inclusio focused on Yahweh as the Creator who provides for all of his creation and the one whose activity did not cease at creation (vv. 5a–9a) but continues in his sustenance of his creation (v. 25a).[84] Furthermore, the linking of these two passages also indicates that Yahweh's provision for his creation qualifies as one of his נפלאות גדלות ("great wonders") (v. 4a) just as much as his creation of the world. Indeed, within the context of the psalm, v. 25a is the final example of the great wonders that set Yahweh apart from other gods (v. 4a).[85]

The connections of v. 25a with previous verses are not limited to vv. 5a–9a. The verb נתן ("give") joins vv. 25a and 21a. Yahweh's gift of food to all creatures is akin to his gift of the land to his servant Israel (vv. 21a–22a). The phonological parallelism between נחלה ("inheritance") (vv. 21a–22a)

---

82. Hossfeld and Zenger, *Psalms*, 509.

83. Auffret, "Note," 8; McCann, *NIB*, 4:1224.

84. Hossfeld and Zenger, *Psalms*, 509. Kimḥi (*Commentary*, 79) connects this verse to the refrain: "It is (an act of) great *loving kindness* from him to (his) creatures, in that he provides for every single creature its appropriate food."

85. Cohen (*The Psalms*, 446) notes in a similar way: "In explaining the proximity to verses 13ff., Rabbi Elazar ben Azariah remarked: 'A man's sustenance is as difficult [to provide] as the dividing of the Red Sea.' i.e., the fact that everyone is provided for is considered miraculous. (Tal. Pes. 118a)." Hengstenberg (*Commentary*, 476) connects it to his care for his people: "The goodness of God to all flesh, in ver. 25, shows that He cannot possibly leave his chosen in humiliation and distress."

and לחם ("bread") (v. 25a) reinforces this link. Whereas the lexical parallel emphasizes Yahweh's similar actions toward both groups (i.e., Israel and all creatures), the phonological parallelism between נחלה and לחם draws out the differences. Yahweh gives the bare necessities to all creatures, but an inheritance to his people.

Concluding Call to Thanksgiving (v. 26)

The final verse of Ps 136 restates the imperative הודו ("give thanks") that last appeared in v. 3a and that governed all the verses within the body of the psalm (vv. 4–25). Verse 26a is therefore the second part of the imperatival inclusio around the psalm.[86] As in vv. 1a–3a, a divine name with a prefixed lamed preposition follows the imperative in v. 26a. The divine name employed (אל השמים ["God of the heavens"]) parallels the name used in v. 2a (אלהים ["God"]). This divine name only appears here in the Psalter, occurring most often in postexilic texts.[87]

A key issue revolving around the use of this divine name is its meaning. Ḥakham gives three possibilities: 1) "God who dwells in heaven," 2) "God who rules in heaven," or 3) "God who created the heavens."[88] It may be that each of Ḥakham's options is in some way at work in this title.[89] Yet, there may also be another emphasis related to this phrase: Yahweh's superiority over other gods. Such is the accent in Ps 115 where Yahweh's position in heaven sets him apart from both the idols and men (Ps 115:2–4, 15–16).[90] In fact, Ps 115:3 links Yahweh's position in heaven with his ability to act according to his pleasure. Both his creation of the heavens and his position in heaven separate him from the gods of the earth, i.e., gods made by men whose dwelling place is the earth (Ps 115:4, 16).

The parallels between v. 26a and vv. 2a–3a provide further confirmation for this interpretation since the divine titles in vv. 2a and 3a both underscore Yahweh's superiority over other gods. Hence, the command to give thanks to Yahweh centers on his supremacy over all the so-called gods. In addition, the parallel with v. 5a (which contains the only other reference to

---

86. The same features that distinguish v. 1a from vv. 2a–3a also distinguish it (v. 1a) from the second part of the inclusio (v. 26a).
87. Anderson, *Psalms 73–150*, 896; Allen, *Psalms 101–150*, 299.
88. Ḥakham, *Psalms 101–150*, 380.
89. This may explain why Ḥakham (ibid.) did not choose one of them over the others.
90. Cf. Jonah 1:9.

השמים ["the heavens"] in this psalm) further supports this interpretation. Since he made them, he certainly has the prerogative to rule from them.

Goldingay and Kimḥi both note the thematic significance of the juxtaposition of this verse and v. 25a. The former attaches the universal nature of כל־בשר ("all flesh") to this title by stating, "Yhwh is not merely the God of Israel but the God of the heavens who is the God of all flesh."[91] Such an understanding does accord well with many of the other biblical occurrences of this title.[92] Kimḥi, moving a slightly different direction, relates the title to the rain that comes from heaven and waters all the vegetation.[93]

---

91. Goldingay, *Psalms 90–150*, 596.
92. See Ezra 1:2; Neh 1:4; Dan 2:18.
93. Kimḥi, *Commentary*, 79.

3

Poetic Analysis of Psalm 137

OUTLINE

I. The Sorrow of Remembering Zion While in Babylon (vv. 1–4)

    A. Grief at the Memory of Zion (vv. 1–2)

    B. Foreign Soil is No Place for Zion Songs (vv. 3–4)

II. An Oath of Allegiance to Jerusalem (vv. 5–6)

III. Prayer for Judgment on the Enemies of Jerusalem (vv. 7–9)

    A. Prayer for Yahweh to Remember the Sons of Edom (v. 7)

    B. Blessing on the Destroyer of Babylon (vv. 8–9)

POETIC ANALYSIS

Many psalms are teeming with emotive language, but few psalms can compare to Ps 137. From beginning to end, this psalm reflects the raw emotion of the psalmist (and his companions), moving from deep grief (vv. 1–4) to ultimate joy (vv. 5–6) to vengeful anger (vv. 7–9).

On a literary level, this psalm is set apart by "its strong sensitivity to sounds" and richness "in auditory devices."[1] The writer of this psalm was in every respect a master poet, reflecting his emotions through a

---

1. Bar Efrat, "Love of Zion, 10.

masterful composition full of guttural and sibilant sounds, "word plays and alliterations,"[2] and brilliant imagery. Regarding this psalm's rhythm,[3] Delitzsch states that it "is so expressive that scarcely any Psalm is so easily impressed on the memory as this, which is so pictorial even in sound."[4] Since the psalm consists "largely of prose fitted into some sort of poetic form,"[5] its parallels (outside the phonological level) are primarily vertical (i.e., between cola of different lines), not horizontal (i.e., within the bi-colon/tri-colon).

The psalm consists of the three stanzas corresponding to the three different emotional experiences (see above) of the psalmist:[6] 1) vv. 1–4, 2) vv. 5–6, and 3) vv. 7–9. These three stanzas move from a past to present to future perspective,[7] and each one ends "with a preposition (עַל or אֶל) followed by one or two nouns."[8] The first and last stanzas focus on the enemies of Jerusalem while the middle stanza is concerned only with Jerusalem. Regarding the difference between the first and last stanzas, the former is about the exiles' grief in Babylon, but the latter is a prayer of judgment against Jerusalem's enemies. Remembrance is the dominant motif that binds all three stanzas together.[9]

The Sorrow of Remembering Zion While in Babylon (vv. 1–4)

Several structurally significant features distinguish the first stanza of Ps 137 from the rest of the psalm. First, the 1cp ending נוּ- ("us") appears nine times in the first three verses. Even though this ending is absent from v. 4, the 1cp speech continues in this verse as evidenced by its first verb נשיר ("we sing"). Hence, there are a total of ten "we/us" references in these four verses. A second reason for the distinction of this section is that it "projects

---

2. Ḥakham (*Psalms 101–150*, 392–93) lists all the word plays and alliterations.

3. This psalm is a favorite for those who practice syllable counting. See Halle and McCarthy, "Metrical Structure"; Freedman, "The Structure"; Shea, "Qinah Meter"; and Renfroe, "Persiflage."

4. Delitzsch, *Commentary*, 332.

5. Renfroe, "Persiflage," 527.

6. For a good survey of structural options, see Allen, *Psalms 101–150*, 305–6.

7. Ḥakham, *Psalms 101–150*, 391.

8. Bar Efrat, "Love of Zion," 4.

9. The root זכר appears in vv. 1, 6, and 7. Its antonym (שכח) is found twice in v. 5.

Poetic Analysis of Psalm 137

a vivid topogaphy of the exilic situation"[10] by means of three על clauses, על נהרות בבל ("by the rivers of Babylon") (v. 1), על־ערבים ("upon the poplars") (v. 2), and על אדמת נכר ("upon foreign soil") (v. 4). The על clauses in vv. 1 and 4 form an inclusio around this opening section of the psalm.[11]

In addition to this inclusio, Goldingay identifies two inner frames.[12] First, the weeping of v. 1 contrasts with the singing of v. 4. Second, he highlights the two references to Zion at the end of vv. 1 and 3. Additionally, Allen, based on the word play between תלינו ("we hung") (v. 2) and תוללינו ("our tormentors") (v. 3), refers to the links within this section (vv. 1–4) as "signs of chiasm."[13]

This first stanza consists of two strophes that are distinct on both the thematic and lexical levels: 1) vv. 1–2 and 2) vv. 3–4. Thematically, the first (vv. 1–2) gives primacy to the location of the exiles (underscored by two על-fronted clauses) and their pathos, while vv. 3–4 present the interchange between the captors (v. 3) and their captives (v. 4). Lexically, vv. 3–4 differ based on the numerous occurrences of the root שיר ("sing" or "song") (zero occurrences in vv. 1–2 versus five appearances in vv. 3–4). Phonologically, the two strophes are dissimilar on the basis of the dominance of labials in vv. 1–2.[14] Also, the ten "we/us" references of this stanza (vv. 1–4) are distributed evenly across these two strophes, five times in each.[15]

Grief at the Memory of Zion (vv. 1–2)

The opening verse of Ps 137 is a tri-colon with an accent count of 3 + 3 + 2. The presence of שם ("there") at the beginning of v. 1b, the antecedent of which is נהרות בבל ("rivers of Babylon") in v. 1a, signals the separation of v.1a and b. The use of the pronoun in v. 1b indicates a poetic pause between בבל ("Babylon") (v. 1a) and שם ("there") (v. 1b).[16] The division of v. 1b and

---

10. Hossfeld and Zenger, *Psalms*, 514.
11. Ibid., 513.
12. Goldingay, *Psalms 90–150*, 602.
13. Allen, *Psalms 101–150*, 306.
14. Freedman, "The Structure," 307. Verse 3 is dominated by sibilants and v. 4 by gutturals.
15. Fokkelman, *Major Poems*, 2:301.
16. Many cite this pronoun as evidence for a postexilic composition of Ps 137 (example.g., Segert, "Poetry and Arithmetic," 167). For a discussion of different options for the date of composition, see Allen, *Psalms 101–150*, 304. Berlin ("Psalms and the Literature of Exile," 67) points out that regardless of the speakers' location, "the sense of

c is based on two factors. First, perfect verbs, which also rhyme, unite the two clauses within v.1b. Second, the infinitive construct at the beginning of v. 1c reinforces this division because it defines the timing of the actions of v. 1b. Consequently, the progression of v. 1 can be outlined by three adverbial questions: "where" (v. 1a), "what" (v. 1b), and "when" (v. 1c).

The initial prepositional phrase of v. 1a identifies the location of the people's actions in v. 1b. The fronting of this prepositional phrase (within the verse and also the psalm) underscores the dire conditions of the exile.[17] The people of Israel were no longer near Jerusalem, but were, as v. 4 will further clarify, in a foreign nation under the control of their captors. Thus, as the reader moves from v. 1a to v. 1b, the actions of the people in v. 1b come as no surprise; they were doing just as expected.

The reference to the נהרות בבל ("rivers of Babylon") is consistent with the portrait of Babylon given in other portions of Scripture.[18] The reference to Babylon's rivers is an example of synecdoche. Augustine sums it up well when he writes, "[T]he rivers are mentioned as a characteristic feature of the country, just as we might speak of the mountains of Switzerland or the plains of Tartary, meaning Switzerland or Tartary itself."[19]

Verse 1b moves the thought of the tri-colon one step further (i.e., syntagmatic parallelism) by describing the actions of the captors in the land of Babylon. It contains two clauses. The first describes the posture of the exiles (ישבנו ["we sat"]) and the second their grief (בכינו ["we wept"]). These two actions (sitting and weeping) often appear together in biblical texts related to mourning.[20] The captives' sitting was therefore an external picture of the posture of their souls. The people were burdened with grief and anguish. Such emotion is made explicit in the second clause of this colon.

The psalmist's choice of שם ("there") and גם ("yea") in the second colon is significant because neither lexeme is required on the semantic level.[21] As previously noted, the presence of שם ("there") at the beginning of this colon creates a division between v. 1a and b. Also, its position (immediately after its antecedent) indicates that it is being used emphatically, thus giving

---

alienation remains the same." In the end, its context within Book V of the Psalter gives it a postexilic perspective.

17. Bar Efrat, "Love of Zion," 4.
18. Cf. Jer 51:13; Ezek 1:1; 3:15; and Dan 8:2.
19. Augustine, *Expositions*, 534.
20. Cf. Judg 20:26; 2 Sam 12:21; and Jon 3:6–7 (uses זעק instead of בכה).
21. Bar Efrat, ("Love of Zion," 4) refers to "the (redundant) particle שם."

"prominence to the place of sojourn."²² Like שׁ ("there"), גם ("also" or "yea") is not essential since the psalmist could have chosen the more common ו ("and"). Although one could understand גם ("also") simply as an alternative to (and thus synonymous with) ו ("and"), its connections with שׁ ("there") point toward a phonological motivation and an emphatic function.²³ Thus, it serves the purpose of "introducing a climax"²⁴ and should be translated "yea."²⁵

The particle גם ("yea") underscores the climatic action, i.e., the people's weeping (בכינו ["we wept"]). This final verb carries the weight of this verse's pathos. If one views their sitting in isolation, one could interpret it either positively or negatively. However, the use of verb בכה ("weep") ensures a negative interpretation. The deep pain and grief of the exiles comes to the fore with this verb.

Extensive parallels between this second colon and v. 1a are non-existent because of the syntagmatic nature of the verse. Yet, Hengstenberg notes a possible parallel between נהרות ("rivers") in v. 1a and בכינו ("we wept") in v. 1b. He writes, "The children of Israel placed themselves beside the streams of Babylon because they saw in them the image and symbol of their floods of tears."²⁶

Verse 1c continues the progression of the verse's thought by indicating the reason for the people's grievous state. The stimulus of their anguish was their memory of Zion; indeed, they were homesick. On the level of the psalm, both items in this colon are unique. First, the infinitive phrase בזכרנו ("when we remembered") represents the psalm's only infinitive.²⁷ Second, the direct object marker is found only here and in v. 6c.

The mention of Zion at the end of the verse establishes a contrast with the beginning of the verse, a contrast between where the people were (על נהרות בבל ["by the rivers of Babylon"]) and where they longed to be (ציון

---

22. Hengstenberg, *Commentary*, 480. Cf. Delitzsch, *Commentary*, 332; Ḥakham, *Psalms 101-150*, 387.

23. Ḥakham (*Psalms 101-150*, 387) identifies "a sort of rhyme, or play on words, or alliteration." Savran ("'How Can We Sing," 45) terms שׁ and גם "assonant helping word[s]."

24. BDB, 169.

25. HALOT, 1:196.

26. Hengstenberg, *Commentary*, 480. Cf. Ḥakham, *Psalms 101-150*, 387. Bar Efrat ("Love of Zion," 5) contrasts the rivers with "Zion" (v. 1c), a place which "evokes dryness."

27. This infinitival phrase בזכרנו has two phonological parallels with v. 1b: בכינו and ישבנו.

["Zion"]). This contrast also evokes the pronoun שָׁם ("there") in v. 1b. They were "there" in that captive land of rivers and not at home in Zion.[28]

The spotlight remains on the people's location in v. 2. This verse is a bi-colon with an accent count of 2 + 2. For the most part, the two cola of v. 2 parallel the first two cola of v. 1. As with v. 1ab, the parallelism between these two cola is strictly syntagmatic since the verse reads like a sentence. Like v. 1ab, v. 2a describes the "where" and v. 2b explains the "what."

The repetition of the preposition עַל ("upon") at the beginning of v. 2 is an example of the psalmist's use of anaphora to continue his vigorous focus on the people's location.[29] Semantically, the עַל of v. 2a has a slightly different meaning than the עַל of v. 1a. In v. 1a, it carries the idea of being "along, beside" something, whereas in v. 2a, it expresses the notion of being "on, upon" something.[30] In v. 1a, the prepositional phrase notes the location of the people; in v. 2a, the place of their lyres.

The object of the preposition (עֲרָבִים [poplars]) parallels the object of the preposition in v. 1a (נְהָרוֹת ["rivers"]) since both describe the topography of Babylon. Since willow trees often appear on riverbanks, the lexical pairing of these two nouns may be the result of what Berlin terms "conventionalized coordinates."[31]

Last, the final words of vv. 1a and 2a exhibit several correspondences. The prepositional phrase of v. 2a (בְּתוֹכָהּ ["in its midst"]) is linked with בָּבֶל ("Babylon") (v. 1a) (the latter is the antecedent of the pronoun in the former). The noun (v. 1a) and the pronoun (v. 2a) both give further clarification as to the location of the rivers and willows. They are not just in any land; they are in the land of Babylon. So, in many respects the prepositional phrase at the end of v. 2a functions similarly to the pronoun at the beginning of v. 1b (שָׁם ["there"]). Its absence would not necessarily affect the meaning of v. 2a (the location of the exiles has been clear since the first words of the psalm); yet, its presence drives home the psalmist's primary emphasis of these opening verses: the people were exiled "in the midst" of Babylon!

Verse 2b supplies the verb that governs the adverbial clause of v. 2a. It describes what the people did "on the poplars" of Babylon, i.e., they hung

---

28. Ḥakham (*Psalms 101–150*, 387) posits the possibility that צִיּוֹן may be an allusion to צִיָּה. This latter word would also contrast with "rivers" at the beginning of the verse.

29. Fokkelman, *Major Poems*, 2:301.

30. Ḥakham (*Psalms 101–150*, 387) cites Gen 41:1 as a parallel to its usage in v. 1.

31. Berlin, *Dynamics*, 76. Ḥakham (*Psalms 101–150*, 387) cites Lev 23:40 for support.

their musical instruments (כנרותינו ["our lyres"]). The image of hanging up instruments "once used to accompany the songs of praise" aptly illustrates the internal anguish of the exiles.[32] Such an action "signifies publicly (and before God?) that one has given up praise."[33] The cessation of joyful song parallels the sitting and weeping of v. 1b.[34] Semantically, the meaning of the two actions is very similar. Verse 1b emphasizes their grief while v. 2b "gives a concrete picture" of their grief.[35] As their joy turned to mourning, the exiles' lyres found a home in the trees, "idle" and "silent."[36]

Foreign Soil is No Place for Zion Songs (vv. 3–4)

This second strophe continues the 1cp ("we/us") perspective of vv. 1–2 (five 1cp references), but moves beyond the topography of the land of Babylon to the Babylonians. In particular, these verses record the dialogue between the captors and the captives, a dialogue that revolves around singing (five occurrences of the root שיר ["sing"]).

The first verse (v. 3) of this strophe contains the captors' request for a song. The numerous sibilants at the beginning of words display alliteration across the five cola of this verse.[37] In spite of its length (5 cola; 12 words), its contents make its division relatively natural. The first line of the verse is a tri-colon in which the speakers (1cp) describe the captors' request with an indirect quotation (v. 3abc). The second line is a bi-colon that contains a direct quotation of the captors' words (v. 3de).

The tri-colon of v. 3 has an accent count of 3 + 2 + 2. The initial colon (v. 3a) leaves readers with two questions: 1) who asked (subject), and 2) for what did they ask (indirect object)? V. 3b and c, both of which supply a subject and object for the verb of v. 3a, answer these two questions. Therefore, of the three cola, the parallelism between v. 3b and c is the greatest.

The opening כי ("for") connects this strophe with the first strophe (vv. 1–2). It gives a more specific reason (in addition to their remembrance of Zion in v. 1c) for the exiles' mourning and cessation of praise (vv. 1–2),

---

32. Barnes, *Notes*, 282.

33. Goldingay, *Psalms 90–150*, 604. He also notes that "the vast majority of references to lyres connect them with praise."

34. The twofold occurrence of the 1cp ending in each colon reinforces this connection.

35. Bar Efrat, "Love of Zion," 6.

36. Allen, *Psalms 101–150*, 307.

37. Watson, *Classical*, 226.

Part 1: The Poetry of Psalms 135–137

viz., their captors wanted them to sing songs, and not just any songs, but the "songs of Zion" (v. 3e). In this regard, v. 3 shows that the exiles' remembrance of Zion (v. 1c) was not always voluntary but was sometimes brought about by their captors' taunts.

The שם ("there") of v. 3a again emphasizes the exiles' undesirable location. Like its previous appearance in v. 1b, it is not essential for a proper understanding of the verse since vv. 1–2 have made the exiles' location clear. Its occurrence here marks the fourth reference to Babylon in the first three verses of the psalm.

As with the previous two verses, v. 3a moves from the "where" (שם ["there"]) to the "what" (שאלונו) ["asked us"]. The verbal clause שאלונו ("asked us") governs v. 3b and c. This verb (3mp) contrasts in person with the previous three verbs (1cp).[38] For the first time in the psalm, the exiles are not the actors, but the recipients of the action.

With v. 3b and c, one encounters a rarity in this psalm: strong parallelism between two cola within a bi-colon/tri-colon.[39] Lexically, the subjects as well as the objects parallel one another. In both cases, the second member of each pair gives a more definitive description of the nature of the first. The subjects are co-referents, both referring to the captors. The description of the Babylonians as תוללינו ("our tormentors") (v. 3c) underscores how they treated the people.[40] In addition, the object שמחה ("gladness") (v. 3c) clarifies the exact nature of the דברי־שיר ("words of a song") (v. 3b) the captors requested the exiles to sing.[41] Thus, v. 3c clarifies v. 3b and is an example of what Berlin terms "disambiguation."[42]

The second part of v. 3 is a short bi-colon that has an accent count of 2 + 2 and consists of the direct speech of the captors to the captives. The semantic parallelism of the two cola is syntagmatic, and the only lexical

---

38. This verbal clause continues the pattern of words ending in נו-.

39. Both cola contribute to the alliteration of sibilant sounds that stretch across the entire verse. Even more important is the word play between תוללינו in v. 3c and תלינו in v. 2b, which associates the exiles' hanging of their instruments with their tormentors. Cf. Goldingay, *Psalms 90–150*, 599.

40. Of the two terms that describe the Babylonians in v. 3b and c, the first (שובינו) is the more neutral term and does not necessarily imply harsh treatment. The second term (תוללינו) highlights such harsh and oppressive treatment. Cf. Savran, "How Can We Sing," 47; Goldingay, *Psalms 90–150*, 604.

41. Cf. Hengstenberg, *Commentary*, 481.

42. Berlin, *Dynamics*, 96.

parallel is the repetition of the root שיר ("sing" or "song") in both cola (verb in v. 3d; noun in v. 3e).[43]

Since this verse is a direct quotation of the captors' request, it continues the thought of the previous tri-colon. For example, the verb of v. 3a (שאל ["asked"]) governs the verb of v. 3d (שירו ["sing"]), since the latter represents the content of their request. Yet, the verb of v. 3d also clarifies the manner of their asking (v. 3a). The use of the imperative (v. 3d) increases the forceful connotations of the verb שאל ("ask") in v. 3a. In other words, it was probably more of a demand than a request.[44]

The parallels of v. 3d with the previous tri-colon are not limited to v. 3a but also extend to v. 3b and c. In addition to the sibilant alliteration, the verb of v. 3d (שירו ["sing"]) parallels the noun form of this same root in v. 3b (שיר ["song"]). The prepositional phrase of v. 3d (לנו ["to us"]) is made up of a sequence of consonants that is present not only in v. 3a and c (שאלונו ["asked us"] in v. 3a; תוללינו ["our tormentors"] in v. 3c) but also in v. 2 (תלינו ["we hung"]). Furthermore, v. 3a, b, and d all have a word beginning with שׁ and ending with ו (שאלונו ["asked us"] in v. 3a; שובינו ["our captors"] in v. 3b; שירו ["sing"] in v. 3d), thus creating a harmony of sounds in a verse where the sound of music was intended as a taunt for the captives of Israel.

Verse 3e informs the reader of the exact type of song the captors wanted their captives to sing for them (i.e. it is the object of the verb); they were to sing משיר ציון ("one of the Zion songs").[45] This identification continues the description of the song the captors desired. Verse 3b gives the method of singing (vocal, not simply instrumental), v. 3c gives the manner by which it is to be sung (joyfully), and v. 3e gives the type/subject of the song (a Zion song).[46]

This colon also parallels v. 3a. The reference to Zion (v. 3e) contrasts with the pronoun שם ("there") (v. 3a), the referent of which is Babylon. In this regard, this verse is similar to v. 1, which also begins with a reference to Babylon and ends with a reference to Zion. Moreover, the lack of a 1cp reference in this colon underscores the contrast between Babylon and Zion. In vv. 1–4, there are only four cola that do not include a 1cp reference: v.

---

43. The first (שירו) and last (ציון) words of this bi-colon continue the pattern of sibilant alliteration (as in v. 3abc).

44. Ḥakham, *Psalms 101–150*, 388.

45. Delitzsch (*Commentary*, 333–34) and Hossfeld and Zenger (*Psalms*, 515) both highlight the partitive meaning of the preposition מן (i.e., "one from the songs of Zion").

46. For the identification of a Zion song, see discussion of v. 4a (below).

1a, v. 2a, v. 3e, and v. 4b. Of these four, v. 3e is unique in that it contains a reference to Zion. So, what is the subject matter of the other three? They are all עַל ("upon") clauses describing the land of Babylon. This 3:1 ratio accentuates the overbearing weight of the captors' land upon the captives.

After outlining the dreadful demand of the Babylonians (v. 3), the psalmist gives the captive's rhetorical response in v. 4, which underscores the perplexity of their captivity comes. Their location symbolized the judgment of Yahweh upon them and consequently merited a response of repentant grief instead of jubilant song.

This verse is a bi-colon with an accent count of 3 + 3 and has syntagmatic parallelism on the semantic level. Yet, in keeping with the established pattern, this verse's parallels with earlier verses far outweigh its internal parallels. Verse 4a is akin to v. 3, and v. 4b to vv. 1–2. Concerning the former, the initial אֵיךְ ("How") of v. 4a echoes the opening כִּי ("for") of v. 3.[47] This reversal of consonants (כִּי → אֵיךְ) mirrors the exchange between the two groups within these verses. Also, the verb of v. 4a (נָשִׁיר ["we sing"]) parallels the imperative form of this same verb in v. 3d (שִׁירוּ ["sing"]).[48] Hence, the people decline to fulfill the demands of the captors.[49] Furthermore, the object of v. 4a (שִׁיר־יְהוָה ["Yahweh song"]), which includes the first reference to Yahweh in this psalm, parallels the object in v. 3e (שִׁיר צִיּוֹן ["Zion song"]) (i.e., they are co-referents).[50] This parallel demonstrates that the songs of Zion were not primarily concerned with a place but with Yahweh. The parallel between these two terms also establishes a contrast in perspectives between the Babylonians (speakers in v. 3de) and the exiles of Israel (speakers in v. 4).[51] They are not simply songs about Israel's homeland

---

47. Fokkelman, *Major Poems*, 2:301.

48. The verb of v. 4a is the only yiqtol verb within this stanza (four qatal verbs in vv. 1–3a).

49. Ḥakham (*Psalms 101–150*, 388) notes that אֵיךְ indicates "absolute refusal."

50. Allen (*Psalms 101–150*, 307), Anderson (*Psalms 73–150*, 898), Briggs (*Commentary*, 485) and Kirkpatrick (*The Book of Psalms*, 781) all identify "Zion songs" and "Yahweh songs" as synonyms.

51. The parallel between these two terms should also serve as a control against reading the modern form-critical category of "hymn/song of Zion" into the term שִׁיר צִיּוֹן (v. 3e). As v. 4 clarifies, these Zion songs are simply "songs composed and used in the worship of Yahweh" (Briggs, *Commentary*, 485; cf. Alter, *Psalms*, 474).

(Babylonian perspective),⁵² but are "sacred music" (exiles' perspective) centered on Yahweh.⁵³

Verse 4b (the final colon of the first stanza) once again identifies the location of the exiles by means of a על ("upon") prepositional phrase.⁵⁴ This phrase marks the fifth and final reference to Babylon in the first stanza of the psalm and clarifies the reason for their refusal to sing a song of Yahweh.⁵⁵ Here, the captives refer to Babylon as אדמת נכר ("foreign soil"), continuing the contrast between Zion and Babylon.⁵⁶ Verse 1 highlights the rivers of Babylon, v. 2 highlights the poplars, and this verse highlights the soil. is highlighted

An Oath of Allegiance to Jerusalem (vv. 5–6)

The psalmist's reflection on the situation in Babylon gives way to his passionate confession of loyalty to Jerusalem in vv. 5–6. Several features distinguish this second stanza from the rest of the psalm. First, there is switch from 1cp speakers (vv. 1–4) to a 1cs speaker (a total of seven "I" references) in these verses. Second, it contains three oaths that are marked by the particle אם ("if") (one in each line) and two self-curses that serve as the apodoses of the oaths, features unique to this stanza.⁵⁷ Third, the addressee of these two verses is Jerusalem (personified) in comparison to the absence of an addressee in vv. 1–4, Yahweh in v. 7, and Babylon in vv. 8–9. Fourth, all the verbs in this section are yiqtol verbs; in contrast, almost all the verbs

---

52. See Savran, "How Can We Sing," 48.

53. Alter, *Psalms*, 474.

54. This phrase, along with the על prepositional phrase in v. 1a, creates an inclusio around the first stanza of this psalm.

55. Commentators devote much attention to the specific theological reason why they could not sing Yahweh songs on foreign soil. Barnes (*Notes*, 284), Weiser (*The Psalms*, 795), and Augustine (*Expositions*, 534) emphasize how singing such a song would be a violation of the exiles' feelings. The emphasis on the exiles' grief in this stanza indicates that it is not a theological question, but an emotional questiom. Cf. Bar Efrat, "Love of Zion," 6.

56. נכר parallels two words in this stanza. First, it echoes כנרותינו of v. 2b (Allen, *Psalms 101–150*, 306), highlighting the uselessness of musical instrumnents in a foreign land. Second, it resonates with the infinitive phrase of v. 1c (בזכרנו), underscoring the reason why they had to remember Zion (i.e., they were in a foreign place).

57. Ḥakham (*Psalms 101–150*, 389) states that these verses have "the form of an 'oath of a curse.' . . . We often find that a person taking such an oath would omit the second part the curse."

in the previous section are qatal verbs.⁵⁸ Fifth, as Fokkelman notes, each verse within this stanza mentions a different body part.⁵⁹ Sixth, the time reference in this stanza is clearly oriented toward the future, in contrast to the past perspective of the first stanza.⁶⁰

This stanza consists of three bi-cola, one in v. 5 and two in v. 6. Of the three, the first two (v. 5ab and v. 6ab) display the most similarities. First, they both have an accent count of 2 + 2, whereas v. 6cd has an accent count of 3 + 3. Second, they both contain an oath and a self-curse in contrast to v. 6cd, which consists only of an oath. Third, they exhibit strong parallels on every linguistic level.

Verse 5a gives both the speaker and the addressee. The speaker is the psalmist who speaks as the exiles' representative.⁶¹ Coupled with the oaths and curses, this first person perspective underscores the "passionate note" of this section.⁶² The switch from the first plural to first singular also indicates a switch from past reflection to present determination.⁶³

The psalmist's addressee is Jerusalem. This is the first mention of Jerusalem in the psalm, but certainly not the last, since it appears in every bi-cola of vv. 5–6 (by name in v. 5ab and 6cd; by pronoun in v. 5cd). The parallel between the memory motif in these verses and v. 1c indicates that Zion (v. 1c) and Jerusalem (vv. 5–6) are co-referents in this psalm.⁶⁴ Accordingly, the latter designation replaces the former in vv. 5–9.

The numerous references to Jerusalem in this section (4x) correspond to the abundant references to Babylon in the previous section (5x). These Jerusalem references complement the pathos and theme of this section perfectly. The terrible experiences of Babylon no longer dominate but have been replaced by joyous (v. 6d) thoughts of Jerusalem.

Verse 5a also introduces the theme of the entire section, viz., not forgetting/remembering Jerusalem. This theme is given in the form of an oath (signaled by אם ["if"]) here and in v. 6. Verses 5a and 6b stress the

---

58. The only exception is the yiqtol of v. 4a.

59. Fokkelman, *Major Poems*, 2:301.

60. Bar Efrat ("Love of Zion," 7) highlights the future outlook of these verses.

61. Allen, *Psalms 101–150*, 308; Delitzsch, *Commentary*, 334.

62. Weiser, *The Psalms*, 796.

63. The switch from qatal verbs (vv. 1–4) to yiqtol verbs (vv. 5–6) may indicate this switch in time perspective. Cf. Hossfeld and Zenger, *Psalms*, 517.

64. Augustine, *Expositions*, 534. Hossfeld and Zenger (*Psalms*, 517) note, "[the] topographical point of reference is no longer called 'Zion,' but 'Jerusalem.'"

Poetic Analysis of Psalm 137

importance of remembering Jerusalem in positive and negative formulations respectively, and v. 6cd elucidates what this remembrance looks like.

Verse 5b provides the curse the psalmist wishes upon himself in the event that he fails to fulfill his vow of v. 5a. This curse is related to the psalmist's right hand (ימיני).[65] Verse 5b parallels v. 5a through the repetition of the verb שכח ("forget"). By repeating this verb, the psalmist associates the actions of the vow and the curse. If Jerusalem ever ceases to cross his mind, he hopes his hand ceases to function.

The bi-colon of v. 6ab is a reversal of v. 5, thus creating a grammatical chiasm (abb'a').[66] The self-curse is stated first and then followed by the oath. Like v. 5b, the self-curse involves a body part, but unlike v. 5b, it mentions two body parts, both of which are components of the mouth. The picturesque description of the tongue sticking to the roof of the mouth stresses the cessation of speech.[67] In this sense, it is similar to the curse evoked upon the hand in v. 5b (semantic parallel).[68] If the psalmist forgets Jerusalem, he hopes his hand and mouth cease their normal functions.

The body parts that the psalmist mentions relate back to the first section in an important manner. Verses 1–4 mention two types of music. Verse 2 focuses on instrumental music (כנרותינו ["our lyres"]) and vv. 3–4 on vocal music (דברי־שיר ["words of a song"]). The hand (v. 5) is essential for the former and the tongue (v. 6) for the latter.[69] This correspondence implies that the psalmist, if he fails to remember Jerusalem, wishes upon himself a physical condition akin to the emotional condition of the exiles in Babylon. The deep grief of their exile prevented the exiles from musical celebration (vv. 1–4). The psalmist prays that, in the case of his forgetting Jerusalem, his physical infirmities would prevent him from musical celebration (vv. 5–6).

When coupled with the memory motif of both sections, these connections also establish a contrast. While in Babylon (vv. 1–4), the *memory* of Zion (v. 1c) caused the exiles to "hang up" their instruments and to give up singing. In vv. 5–6 (location of psalmist not specified), the *forgetting* of

---

65. It is difficult to translate v. 5b because of its awkward construction. Delitzsch (*Commentary*, 334–35) outlines the options. He proposes translating the verb reflexively: "forget itself, or its service . . . which is equivalent to let it refuse or fail."

66. Berlin, *Dymanics*, 86.

67. Anderson (*Psalms 73–150*, 899) cites the parallel passages Ezek 3:26 and Lam 4:4.

68. Several phonological parallels underscore this semantic similarity: 1) the three body parts rhyme (by the י ending), 2) ימיני (v. 5b) and לשוני (v. 6a), and 3) לחכי (v. 6b), אשכחך (v. 5a), and תשכח (v. 5b).

69. Augustine, *Expositions*, 534; Ahn, "Psalm 137," 284; and Alter, *Psalms*, 474.

Jerusalem would cause the psalmist to be incapacitated in a manner that would prevent him from singing and stringing.

Verse 6b consists of an oath that corresponds to the initial oath of this stanza (v. 5a). The lexical and semantic parallelism between these two cola (v. 5a and 6b) is paradigmatic.[70] The presence of the negative particle לֹא ("not") establishes a grammatical contrast between the two cola. Regarding this contrast, Ḥakham states, "The first oath (in verse 5) is formulated in positive terms, but has a negative meaning.... The next two oaths (in verse 6) are formulated in negative terms, but have a positive meaning."[71]

The form of the 2fs suffix attached to the verb of v. 6b (כִי- ["you"]) is exceptional in this psalm.[72] While it could be merely a characteristic of later poetry,[73] the psalmist's seems to have chosen it for other reasons. By utilizing this suffix, the psalmist establishes rhyme across all three bi-cola within this stanza (יְמִינִי ["my right hand"] in v. 5b; אֶזְכְּרֵכִי ["I remember you"] in v. 6b; שִׂמְחָתִי ["my joy"] in v. 6d). It also creates a rhyme between the two cola of this bi-colon (לְחִכִּי ["roof of my mouth"] and אֶזְכְּרֵכִי ["I remember you"])[74] and joins into the rhyme (by means of the final י) already established in the previous two cola.[75] Bar Efrat, commenting on this rhyme across vv. 5–6, argues that "[t]he י-ending ... referring to the speaker [vv. 5b and 6a], and ... referring to Jerusalem [v. 6b], hints at the bond between the speaker and Jerusalem."[76] Once again, the psalmist's masterful use of sounds underscores the rich nuances of meaning in this psalm.

The last bi-colon of this stanza (v. 6cd) explains what it means to remember Jerusalem (vv. 5ab and 6ab),[77] i.e., it means to make Jerusalem one's highest joy.[78] This bi-colon has an accent count of 3 + 3 and its two cola relate to one another syntagmatically. Although it does not contain a curse (like vv. 5 and 6ab), its oath aligns it with the curses of the previous

---

70. The verb of v. 6b (זכר) is the antonym of the verb of v. 5ab (שכח).

71. Ḥakham, *Psalms 101–150*, 389.

72. The more common form appears four times in this psalm: vv. 5, 8 (2x), and 9.

73. Delitzsch (*Commentary*, 335) states, "[T]hese later Psalms are so fond of adorning themselves" with it.

74. Goldingay, *Psalms 90–150*, 600.

75. Fokkelman, *Major Poems*, 2:301.

76. Bar Efrat, "Love of Zion," 8.

77. Goldingay, *Psalms 90–150*, 607.

78. BDB (911) and HALOT (3:1167) support this typical translation/interpretation of רֹאשׁ.

two bi-cola, thus implying that the curse formulae of vv. 5 and 6ab are applicable to this bi-colon.[79]

Verse 6c begins, as v. 5, with the oath-signaling particle אם ("if"), but instead of being grammatically positive, the oath is worded in negatively (אם־לא ["if not"]) as in v. 6b. Verse 6c also contains the verb and the direct object of this bi-colon. The verb (אעלה ["I lift up"]) governs v. 6d, which is an adverbial phrase describing how the psalmist would lift up Jerusalem.

With regard to the stanza as a whole (vv. 5–6), v. 6cd exhibits a couple of connections with the other two bi-cola. First, in addition to the lexical parallels involving אם־לא ("if not"), the proper noun ירושלם ("Jerusalem") relates back to this same noun in v. 5a. Yet, there is one major difference. It functions gramatticaly as a vocative in v. 5a, but here it functions as a direct object. This third person reference to Jerusalem sets v. 6cd apart from vv. 5ab and 6ab. The psalmist is no longer addressing Jerusalem directly, but is speaking about Jerusalem. This serves as further confirmation that the purpose of v. 6cd is to clarify the meaning of the oaths in the previous two bi-cola. A second parallel within this stanza relates to ראש ("cheif"/"head") in v. 6d. Even though this is a metaphorical use of the body part, it parallels the body parts mentioned in vv. 5b and 6a.[80]

This bi-colon's parallels also extend to the first stanza of the psalm (vv. 1–4). The על ("above") prepositional phrase of the second colon (v. 6d) is the fourth and last such prepositional phrase in this psalm. The three על ("upon") prepositional phrases of vv. 1–4 underscore the location of the exiles, but here the focus is not the physical location of the psalmist, but the location of Jerusalem in his affections. The repetition of שמחה ("joy") in both sections (vv. 3c and 6d) reinforces this contrast. He could not give his joy to his captors because he reserved it for Jerusalem.[81]

An even closer inspection reveals that v. 6cd contains several parallels with v. 4. First, Freedman emphasizes that "the sentence structure and sequence of parts of speech are almost identical" in these two bi-cola.[82] Second, the dominance of guttural sounds (six in v. 4 and nine in v. 6cd) links them together. Third, the second colon of each bi-colon begins with the

---

79. Freedman, "Structure," 314.

80. Bar Efrat ("Love of Zion," 8) writes,"This verse [v. 6], which began with parts of the head (tongue and palate), ends with the whole head (in the sense of the highest point)."

81. Cf. Hossfeld and Zenger, *Psalms*, 516.

82. Freedman, "Structure," 311.

preposition עַל ("upon"/"above"). Last, both of these bi-cola have the same accent count (3 + 3) and contain the definite object marker. The purpose of these similarities may be to distinguish these two verses as the concluding verses of their respective stanzas.

Prayer for Judgment on the Enemies of Jerusalem (vv. 7–9)

The final stanza of Ps 137 reintroduces Israel's enemies who seemingly disappeared in the middle stanza (vv. 5–6).[83] As with vv. 1–4, the Babylonians and their atrocities against Jerusalem figure prominently (vv. 8–9). The psalmist also introduces a new enemy, viz., the Edomites (v. 7). The division of this stanza into two strophes (v. 7 and vv. 8–9) accords with the psalmist's focus on each of the enemies of Jerusalem.[84]

A Prayer for Yahweh to Remember the Sons of Edom (v. 7)

The focus of v. 7 on the Edomites distinguishes it from vv. 8–9, which are concerned with the Babylonians. It consists of two bi-cola. Verse 7ab is an imperatival address to Yahweh and v. 7cd quotes the Edomites' words at the time of the Babylonian destruction of Jerusalem.

The initial bi-colon of v. 7 has an accent count of 4 + 3, with the cola paralleling each another syntagmatically. The imperative (זכר ["remember"]) of v. 7a continues the memory motif from the psalm's first two stanzas. Whereas the memory of the previous two strophes related to the exiles (v. 1) and the psalmist himself (vv. 5–6), Yahweh's remembrance is now in view. Like the psalmist's remembrance, Yahweh's remembrance relates to Jerusalem, specifically the "day of Jerusalem." The designation of the addressee as Yahweh separates this verse as the only verse in this psalm explicitly directed to Yahweh.

The mention of Israel's arch nemesis in this initial colon comes seemingly out of nowhere since the psalm has only dealt with the Babylonians up to this point. Yet the psalmist's motivation for dealing with the Edomites becomes clear in the rest of v. 7. Moreover, this mention of the Edomites

---

83. Allen, *Psalms 101–150*, 308. Savran ("How Can We Sing," 55) writes, "[T]he poet shifts from a hypothetical time of happiness . . . to a specific time of sorrow."

84. Goldingay (*Psalms 90–150*, 601) states that "both Edom and Babylon became symbols of oppressive power; perhaps neither term refers to the historical Edom or Babylon."

illuminates the type of memory the psalmist desires for Yahweh to have toward these people. It is not a sorrowful memory (v. 1) or a joyful memory (vv. 5–6), but a memory of recompense and vengeance (v. 7).

Verse 7b gives the specific occasion for which Yahweh was to remember the sons of Edom. The occasion is the "day of Jerusalem," i.e., the day the Babylonians destroyed Jerusalem (as clarified in the subsequent verses). This bi-colon exhibits many similarities with earlier verses. First, it corresponds to the preceding stanza via את (direct object marker) (vv. 6c and 7b) and ירושלם ("Jerusalem") (vv. 5a, 6c, 7b). Second, the presence of the divine name in v. 7a links this verse with v. 4, the only other verse in which the divine name appears. Allen interprets this repetition of the divine name "at the end of the first strophe" (v. 4) and "the beginning of the third" (v. 7) as a frame around the second strophe (vv. 5–6).[85] The presence of את (direct object marker) in vv. 4a and 7b and two phonological parallels in these verses reinforce the frame.[86] Hence, the correction to the predicament of v. 4 is the action of Yahweh requested in v. 7.

Verse 7cd gives a direct quotation of the Edomites's words on the "day of Jerusalem." Consequently, this bi-colon gives more detail regarding the motivation behind and nature of the requested remembrance of Yahweh (v. 7a). In fact, the psalmist tells Yahweh exactly what he should remember about the Edomites. This bi-colon has an accent count of 3 + 3 and exhibits syntagmatic parallelism.[87]

Verse 7c opens with a qal participle that refers back to the sons of Edom in v. 7b and introduces their direct speech. The subsequent twofold repetition of the imperative ערו ("lay bare") expresses (emphatically) the Edomites' desired action upon the city of Jerusalem.[88]

Verse 7d consists of two prepositional phrases that delineate the extent and object of the Edomites' desired destruction. The first prepositional phrase gives the extent of the destruction (עד היסוד) ("unto the foundation"), and the second gives the specific location (בה ["in it"]) of the foundations.

---

85. Allen, *Psalms 101–150*, 306.

86. The phonological parallels are: 1) נכר (v. 4b) and זכר (v. 7a), and 2) אדמת (v. 4b) and אדום (v. 7a).

87. One of the prominent features of v. 7cd is its guttural alliteration. Also, the twofold ערו (v. 7c) resonates with ירושלם (v. 7b). Hossfeld and Zenger (*Psalms*, 519) write, "[I]t seems certain that the assonance of 'ārū-yerū could not have been missed."

88. Anderson (*Psalms 73–150*, 900), Briggs (*Commentary*, 486), and Bar Efrat ("Love of Zion," 8–9) note the emphasis attained through the repetition of this imperative.

When one evaluates the connections between v. 7cd and previous stanzas, the correspondence between the direct quotations of v. 7cd and v. 3de stands out.[89] In both instances, the quotation is from the enemies of Jerusalem, contains an imperative, and carries connotations of mocking and derision. The time (during the exile) of the first quotation (v. 3de) is subsequent to the time (during the Babylonian siege of Jerusalem) of the second (v. 7cd). The ר-ו grouping in the imperatives of the first cola (ערו ["lay bare"] in v. 7c; שירו ["sing"] in v. 3d) reinforces the correlation of these two quotations.

The preposition עד ("unto") + location in v. 7d links back to the four earlier instances of the preposition על ("upon") + location. Along with the first three על ("upon") prepositional phrases (vv. 1a, 2a, and 4b), this one "is literal, points downward and causes sadness; that of strophe 3 [v. 6d] is figurative, points upward and is in a major key."[90] In contrast to the psalmist's vow to place Jerusalem as his *highest* joy (v. 6cd), the Edomites yearn for the city's *lowest* parts to be exposed (v. 7cd). The fulfillment of Edom's desire (v. 7cd) led to the Israelite's deportation to a location (v. 1a, 2a, and 4b) that caused great grief.

The parallel between the preposition ב + the feminine pronominal suffix in v. 7d (בה ["in it"]) and בתוכה ("in the midst of it") in v. 2a reinforces the correlation between the prepositional phrases in vv. 7d (עד ["unto"]) and 2a (על ["upon"]).[91] The antecedent of the pronoun in v. 2a is Babylon; the antecedent of the pronoun in v. 7d is Jerusalem. This once again stresses the contrast between Zion/Jerusalem and Babylon.

Blessing on the Destroyer of Babylon (vv. 8–9)

The opening reference to Babylon in v. 8 signals a shift in the psalmist's focus. After expressing his thoughts about Edom, he now turns his attention to Babylon, the enemy who dominated vv. 1–4. In switching enemies, the psalmist does not miss a beat in regard to his desires for them. Although these two sections differ grammatically and stylistically, their focus is the same. If Jerusalem is the psalmist's highest joy, then these verses give his second highest joy: vengeance on Jerusalem's enemies.

---

89. Cf. Allen, *Psalms 101–150*, 306, and Fokkelman, *Major Poems*, 2:302.
90. Fokkelman, *Major Poems*, 2:302.
91. Allen, *Psalms 101–150*, 306.

Poetic Analysis of Psalm 137

Verse 8 is a tri-colon with an accent count of 2 + 2 + 3.[92] It opens with a vocative address to בת־בבל ("Daughter of Babylon").[93] Verse 8b and c include the psalmist's direct address to Babylon, in which he pronounces blessing (אשרי) upon the one who takes vengeance on them for their actions against Jerusalem.[94] On the semantic level, these two cola exhibit syntagmatic parallelism.[95] Simply put, the two cola are a single sentence. Lexically, the two verbs (שׁלם ["recompense"] in v. 8b; גמל ["did"] in v. 8c) are synonymous expressions of recompense or repayment.[96] The direct object גמול ("retribution") (v. 8c), which comes from the same verbal root as the verb in the same colon, reinforces a synonymous interpretation.[97]

With regard to v. 8's connections with previous verses, the designation of Babylon as בת־בבל ("Daughter of Babylon") is significant in the present stanza (vv. 7–9). First, it parallels the label of Edom in v. 7b as בני אדום ("sons of Edom"), thus associating the two enemies of Jerusalem with each other by means of familial terms.[98] Second, v. 9 makes it clear that this daughter also has children (עלליך) who are the objects of repayment.[99] Last, there is also a possibility that the psalmist portrays Jerusalem as a woman in the quotation of the Edomites in v. 7de. Ḥakham notes that the Edomites' command "may be alluding to the image of Jerusalem as a woman ('the daughter Jerusalem,' 'the virgin daughter of Zion') whose enemies, those who take her captive, maltreat her and strip her of clothing and present her naked and bare."[100] If Ḥakham's insight is correct, then every line within this stanza has some kind of familial reference just as the psalm's middle

---

92. Fokkelman (*Major Poems*, 2:302) notes that the verses that begin with Babylon are tri-colic.

93. This phrase is simply a reference to the nation of Babylon. See Ḥakham, *Psalms 101–150*, 390.

94. Hossfeld and Zenger (*Psalms*, 520) (because of the parallels to v. 7) and Ahn ("Psalm 137," 288) (based on Pss 135:8, 10 and 136:23) identify the unmentioned actor of vv. 8–9 as Yahweh.

95. A sound similarity strengthens the close relationship of these verbs: ישלם (v. 8b) and גמלת (v. 8c). See also לך (v. 8b) and את־גמולך (v. 8c).

96. See BDB, 168, 1022.

97. Savran ("How Can We Sing," 57) notes that this verse and vv. 3–4 are the only places in the psalm where "the same root" is used "for both verb and object."

98. Ḥakham, *Psalms 101–150*, 390.

99. Ibid.; Hossfeld and Zenger, *Psalms*, 520.

100. Ḥakham (*Psalms 101–150*, 390) cites the parallel passages Ezek 16:39 and Hos 2:5.

stanza (vv. 5–6) contains references to body parts. Also, the two "women" (Babylon explicitly and Jerusalem implicitly) of this section continue the contrast between Zion/Jerusalem and Babylon.

Furthermore, the personification of Babylon in verse 8 is akin to the personification of Jerusalem in vv. 5–6. In this earlier stanza, the psalmist expresses his positive affections toward Jerusalem negatively (i.e., self-curses); here, the psalmist (or the group of which he is a part) expresses his negative wishes toward Babylon positively (i.e., blessings).[101]

The reference to בת־בבל ("Daughter of Babylon") in v. 8 also connects these last two verses to the first stanza of the psalm (vv. 1–4), which also began with a reference to Babylon (v. 1). Consequently, these Babylonian references serve as a frame around the entire psalm. The five references to Babylon contained in each of these stanzas strengthens their close relationshipby the contained in each section.[102] In vv. 1–4, the five references are to the geographical area associated with Babylon, but those in vv. 8–9 are all references to the personified Babylon.

Ḥakham has highlighted the relationship between the passive participle השדודה ("the one destined to be destroyed") in v. 8a and the qal participle שובינו ("our captors") of v. 3b.[103] The verbal roots of the participles express similar ideas, yet the passive voice of the participle in v. 8a actually produces a contrast. Since Babylon is the subject of both participles, this contrast is between who Babylon was during the exile (captors) and who Babylon will be when the psalmist's prayer is answered (destroyed ones).

The parallels with earlier verses do not cease with v. 8a; v. 8b has a significant phonological parallel with v. 7. The verb ישלם ("recompenses") links back to ירושלם ("Jerusalem") in v. 7 (also with the other two occurrences of ירושלם ["Jerusalem"] in vv. 5–6) by means of the י-ש-ל-ם sequence. This extensive consonance clarifies the exact reason why the psalmist wanted vengeance on the Babylonians. The desired retribution (שלם) relates to the city of Jerusalem, specifically the יום ירושלם ("day of Jerusalem") (v. 7c).[104]

---

101. Fokkelman (*Major Poems*, 2:302) writes, "[T]he open request for retribution remains at the level of advanced rhetoric by wrapping the most terrible monstrosities in a double 'šre."

102. I have already highlighted the five references in vv. 1–4 (see above). The five references in vv. 8–9 are as follows: 1) בת־בבל (v. 8a), 2) 2fs pronoun (v. 8b), 3) 2fs pronoun (v. 8c), 4) 2fs verb (v. 8c), and 5) 2fs pronoun (v. 9b).

103. Ḥakham, *Psalms 101–150*, 393.

104. Hossfeld and Zenger (*Psalms*, 519) write of this word play, "In contrast to the common association that explains Jerusalem as a city of . . . [peace], here the perspecitve

POETIC ANALYSIS OF PSALM 137

In addition to this parallel with v. 7, the אשרי ("blessed") of v. 8b reiterates the sounds of the lexeme שיר ("sing"/"song") that occurs five times in vv. 1–4.[105] In vv. 1–4, the Babylonian captors tormented their captives by commanding song; in v. 8b, the Jerusalemites pronounce blessing on the one who torments the Babylonians by destroying them.

Finally, v. 8c connnects with the first stanza of the psalm (vv. 1–4) by means of the preposition + suffixed pronoun at the end of this verse (לנו ["to us"]). This prepositional phrase is also found in v. 3d.[106] In v. 3d, the antecedent of the pronoun is the taunting Babylonians. In v. 8, the antecedent is the group of Jerusalemites represented by the psalmist. By connecting the recompense of the Babylonians (v. 8) with their taunting requests (v. 3), the psalmist may be indicating that his request for recompense is not simply based on the Babylonian destruction of Jerusalem (v. 8) but also on their subsequent treatment of the exiles in Babylon (v. 3).[107]

Verse 9 continues the psalmist's address to Babylon by giving a specific example of the extent of his requested recompense.[108] The vengeance would be so extensive that even the children within Babylon would suffer a dreadful fate.[109] This verse is a bi-colon with an accent count of 3 + 2. The two cola parallel each other syntagmatically, with v. 9a supplying the subject and verbs and v. 9b supplying the direct object and an adverbial prepositional phrase.[110]

This verse does have a few parallels with v. 8. Semantically, v. 9 is a specification of v. 8cd. Lexically, v. 9a repeats verbatim the initial אשרי ש- ("blessed is the one who") of v. 8b. In addition, the direct object marker and

---

'city of retaliation' is evoked."

105. Savran, "How Can We Sing," 57.

106. Allen, *Psalms 101–150*, 306.

107. In addition to the repetition of לנו, there are four instances in vv. 1–4 of the ל-נ-ו sequence (תלינו in v. 2b; שאלונו in v. 3a; תוללינו in v. 3c; לנו in v. 3d).

108. Ḥakham, *Psalms 101–150*, 391.

109. Watson (*Classical*, 65) cites the reference to death at the end of the psalm as an indicator of thematic closure. A discussion of the ethical difficulties often associated with v. 9 is beyond the scope of this work. For a discussion of these ethical issues, see Osgood, "Dashing the Little Ones"; Martin, "The Imprecations"; Laney, "Fresh Look"; Jauss, "Fluchpsalmen beten?"; Luc, "Interpreting the Curses"; Day, "Imprecatory Psalms"; and Steenkamp, "Violence and Hatred." For a history of interpretation of this verse, see Risse, "Wohl dem."

110. The parallelism between these two cola is limited to the phonological level, evidenced by the numerous gutturals (3 in v. 9a; 5 in v. 9b) and sibilants (4 in v. 9a; 1 in v. 9b) that span this verse. Within v. 9b, עלליך and הסלע resonate.

79

2fs suffixed pronoun of v. 8c reappear in v. 9b. The major connection between v. 9 and v. 8a is עֹלָלַיִךְ ("your children") (v. 9b) and בַּת־בָּבֶל ("Daughter of Babylon") (v. 8a). Not only do they parallel morphologically (the latter is the antecedent of the suffixed pronoun attached to the former) but both also play a role in the family motif of these verses.[111] The children of v. 9 belong to the בַּת־בָּבֶל ("Daughter of Babylon") of v. 8a.

When one moves outside the final stanza, several connections between this stanza and the first emerge. In fact, Savran argues that "the revenge song in vv. 7–9 is intended to counteract the description of Babylon as successful conqueror in vv. 1–4."[112] For instance, the mention of עֹלָלַיִךְ ("your children") (v. 9b) catapults the reader back to the phonologically similar תוֹלָלֵינוּ ("our tormentors") of v. 3c. This parallel highlights the contrast between Babylon's haughty state (vv. 1–4) and their coming retribution (vv. 8–9).[113]

Additionally, Ḥakham highlights the thematic and phonological parallels between the last (v. 9) and first verse of the psalm. The sole phonological parallel Ḥakham notes is the switch from the עַל ("upon") of v. 1a to לַע (in הַסֶּלַע ["the rock"]) at the end of the psalm (v. 9b).[114] For the thematic parallel, he contrasts the imagery associated with flowing water (v. 1a) with the "gruesome and horrible scene" of v. 9. He writes of the "[r]ocks that are covered not with water but with the blood of infants who have been dashed against them."[115]

The mention of a rock also echoes the numerous topographical references in vv. 1–4. Therefore, not only does the psalm begin and end with a phonological parallel, but it also begins and ends with a topographical image (rivers in v. 1a; rock in v. 9b).[116] Savran describes this correspondence in the following manner: "The closing phrase . . . denoting the place of recompense comes as a response to the three עַל phrases which describe Baby-

---

111. Ahn, "Psalm 137," 287.

112. Savran, "How Can We Sing," 57.

113. Fokkelman (*Major Poems*, 2:302) states, "In strophe 2 this city was full of *tolalenu*; here, the ʿ*olalayik* are being tackled."

114. To this might be added עֹלָלַיִךְ in v. 9b.

115. Ḥakham, *Psalms 101–150*, 393.

116. Bar Efrat ("Love of Zion," 9–10) states that the rock "serves to indicate dry, infertile land, as in Ezek 26:4, 14." Therefore, "[t]he rock at the end of the psalm . . . functions as an antithesis to the waters at the beginning. The psalm begins and ends with Babylon, but, whereas at the beginning Babylon was characterized by abundance of water, at the end it has become dry and barren."

lon as the place of Israel's suffering and humiliation in vv. 1–4."[117] These extensive parallels between the first and last stanzas underscore the unity of the psalm and emphatically connect the vengeful tone of vv. 7–9 to the deep grief reflected in vv. 1–4.

---

117. Savran, "How Can We Sing," 57.

Part 2

The Context of Psalms 135–137

4

Contextual Analysis of the Psalm Group 135–137

Since Wilson's work on the editing of the Hebrew Psalter, many students of the Psalms have accepted as a maxim that the canonical context of an individual psalm impacts that psalm's meaning. Hossfeld and Zenger reiterate such sentiment when they note, "[T]he individual psalms are partial texts within the book of Psalms and thus acquire an additional sense space in which they are meant to be heard."[1] The purpose of the next two chapters is to examine this "additional sense space" for Pss 135–137. In order to accomplish this objective, I evaluate the intra-relationship of these psalms (Pss 135–137) in this chapter. In chapter 5, I analyze the group in relation to the two larger psalm groups that bracket it (the Songs of Ascents [Pss 120–134] and the Last Davidic Psalter [Pss 138–145]).

CONNECTIONS WITHIN PSALMS 135–137

In what follows, I examine the lexical, thematic, and structural parallels within the psalm group Pss 135–137. Because of the numerous similarities between Pss 135 and 136, I will first evaluate these two psalms and then compare Pss 135–136 to Ps 137.

---

1. Hossfeld and Zenger, *Psalms*, 513.

PART 2: THE CONTEXT OF PSALMS 135–137

Parallels between Psalms 135 and 136

Due to the excessive amount of parallels between Pss 135 and 136, Hossfeld and Zenger term these two psalms "twin psalms."[2] In fact, one could even argue that a psalmist/editor wrote one of these psalms in light of the other.[3] The lexical parallels between these two psalms alone are enough to convince attentive readers of their intentional placement. Yet, their parallels also extend to the structural and thematic levels.[4] For a list of these parallels, see tables 1–3 below.

Table 1. Structural Parallels between Psalms 135 and 136

Structure	Psalm 135	Psalm 136
Frame (call to praise/bless/give thanks to Yahweh)	vv. 1–4, 19–21	vv. 1–3, 26
Theme Setting Verse of Body	v. 5	v. 4
Proofs of Yahweh's Uniqueness	vv. 6–14	vv. 5–24
Yahweh's Acts of (or in) Creation (Proof 1)	vv. 6–7	vv. 5–9
Yahweh's Acts for His People/Against Their Enemies (Proof 2)	vv. 8–12	vv. 10–22
Yahweh's Care for His People (Proof 3)	vv. 13–14	vv. 23–24

Table 2. Thematic Parallels between Psalms 135 and 136

Psalm 135	Psalm 136
Superiority/Uniqueness of Yahweh (v. 5)	Superiority/Uniqueness of Yahweh (vv. 2–4)
רבים and עצומים (v. 10)	גדלים (v. 17) and אדירים (v. 18)
Yahweh's Care for His People (vv. 13–14)	Yahweh's Care for His People (vv. 23–24)
Pharaoh/Egypt (vv. 8–9); Kings (vv. 10–12)	צרינו (v. 24)
Yahweh's Making of Storms (v. 7)	נתן לחם לכל־בשר (v. 25)

---

2. Hossfeld and Zenger, *Psalms*, 493. For some reason, Zimmerli ("Zwillingspsalmen") does not mention these two psalms.

3. The most likely candidate is Ps 135 because of its "mosaic" character. See poetic analysis of Ps 135 for more details regarding its composite character.

4. Ḥakham, *Psalms 101–150*, 382.

Table 3. Lexical Parallels between Psalms 135 and 136

Psalm 135	Psalm 136
יהוה (vv. 1, 2, 3, 5, 6, 13, 14, 19, 20, 21)	יהוה (v. 1)
כי (vv. 3–5, 14)	כי (v. 1, refrain)
טוב (v. 3)	טוב (v. 1)
לעולם (v. 13)	לעולם (refrain)
אלהים (vv. 2, 5)	אלהים (v. 2)
אדני (v. 5)	אדני (v. 3)
עשׂה (vv. 6, 7, 18); מעשׂה (v. 15)	עשׂה (vv. 4, 5, 7)
גדול (v. 5)	גדול (v. 4, 7, 17)
שׁמים (v. 6)	שׁמים (vv. 5, 26)
ארץ (vv. 6, 7, 12)	ארץ (vv. 6, 21)
ים (v. 6)	ים (vv. 13, 15)
נכה (vv. 8, 10)	נכה (vv. 10, 17)
מצרים (vv. 8, 9)	מצרים (v. 10)
בכור (v. 8)	בכור (v. 10)
יצא (v. 7)	יצא (v. 11)
ישׂראל (vv. 4, 12, 19)	ישׂראל (vv. 11, 14, 22)
תוך (v. 9)	תוך (vv. 11, 14)
יד (v. 15)	יד (v. 12)
פרעה (v. 9)	פרעה (v. 15)
עמו (vv. 12, 14)	עמו (v. 16)
מלך (vv. 10, 11)	מלך (vv. 17, 18, 19, 20)
הרג (v. 10)	הרג (v. 18)
לסיחון מלך האמרי (v. 11)	לסיחון מלך האמרי (v. 19)
ולעוג מלך הבשׁן (v. 11)	ולעוג מלך הבשׁן (v. 20)
נתן (v. 12)	נתן (v. 21, 25)
נחלה (v.12)	נחלה (v. 21, 22)
עבד (vv. 1, 9, 14)	עבד (v. 22)
שׁ (vv. 2, 8, 10)	שׁ (v. 23)
זכר (noun) (v. 13)	זכר (verb) (v. 23)

Part 2: The Context of Psalms 135–137

In what follows, I discuss the key lexical and thematic connections between these two psalms using the structure of Ps 136 as my organizing principle. Several of the lexical parallels in table 3 qualify as what Howard calls "incidental links."[5] Therefore, I will not discuss these words, but will instead focus my attention on key lexical and thematic parallels between these two psalms.[6] Concerning the lexical parallels, I identify important lexical parallels based on three factors: 1) the lexeme's relationship to the major themes of the psalms, 2) the frequency of the lexeme (in the section of the Psalter, the Psalter as a whole, and/or the Hebrew Bible), and 3) the location of the lexeme in the psalm.[7] Since these psalms are "twin psalms," a high precentage of their lexical parallels are significant for interpretation.

The most significant structural difference between Pss 135 and 136 is the refrain in Ps 136 and the lack thereof in Ps 135. Even so, the refrain of Ps 136 echoes Ps 135 lexically and thematically. For example, the initial כי ("for") of the refrain relates back to the threefold appearance of this lexeme in Ps 135:3–4. In each of its occurrences in Ps 135:3–4, it introduces a reason to praise Yahweh. Likewise, the כי ("for") of the refrain serves a similar function in each verse of Ps 136, wherein it gives the primary basis for giving thanks to Yahweh.

The second phrase of the refrain (לעולם ["to forever"]) emphasizes the eternality of Yahweh's loving-kindness (חסד) and parallels the confession of Ps 135:13 (יהוה שמך לעולם ["Yahweh, your name is to forever"]), which underscores the eternality of Yahweh's reputation (שם ["name"]).[8] Hence, Yahweh's acts of loving-kindness toward his people ensure the eternality of his reputation. Psalm 135:14 reinforces this teaching by justifying the psalmist's confession of v. 13. The reasons relate to his vindication of and compassion on his people (i.e., acts of חסד ["loving-kindness"]).

In addition to the parallels between Ps 135 and the refrain of Ps 136, these two psalms have a myriad of other lexical parallels. For instance, the כי ("for") clause of Ps 136:1a (כי־טוב ["for he is good"]) gives the grounds for the initial call to thanksgiving. The same כי ("for") clause (כי־טוב ["for he is good"]) also appears after the command to praise in Ps 135:3. This כי

---

5. Howard, *Structure*, 100. I have included all the lexical parallels in table 3 so readers can make their own decisions regarding the significance of these connections.

6. This will actually be my strategy for all comparisons between psalms and/or psalm groups in the second half of this book.

7. For my justification of these three factors, see the "Research Methodology" section of my "Introduction."

8. The final lexeme in the refrain, חסדו, has no direct parallel in Ps 135.

Contextual Analysis of the Psalm Group 135–137

("for") clause (Ps 135:3), like that of Ps 136:1, represents the first reason for the praise/thanksgiving of Yahweh. Consequently, Yahweh's goodness sets the tone for both psalms.

The two superlative titles in Ps 136:2–3 (אלהי האלהים ["God of gods"]; אדני האדנים ["Lord of lords"]) underscore Yahweh's superiority over other gods. These verses echo Ps 135:5 thematically and lexically. Thematically, both passages express Yahweh's pre-eminence. Lexically, both divine designations in Ps 136:2–3 are present in Ps 135:5. In this latter verse, the psalmsit references Yahweh as אדנינו ("our Lord") and the other gods as אלהים ("gods").[9]

The qal participle of עשה ("the one who does"), which begins Ps 136:4, is the first of three instances of this participle in Ps 136.[10] In a similar manner, the verbal root עשה ("do"/"make") also occurs three times in Ps 135. The first appearance of עשה ("do"/"make") in both psalms has a more general focus, thus undergirding the emphasis on Yahweh's uniqueness. In Ps 135 his ability to *do* what he wants in every part of his creation distinguishes him (v. 6). In Ps 136 the great wonders that he *does* separate him from the competition (v. 4). Hence, Ps 135:6 focuses on the arena (בשמים ובארץ בימים וכל־תהומות ["in the heavens and on the earth, in the seas and all the depths"]) in which, according to Ps 136:4, he does his great wonders.

The second occurrence of עשה ("make") in Ps 135 (v. 7) and the second and third instances of this root in Ps 136 (vv. 5, 7) all address Yahweh's creative work. Psalm 135:7 underscores his present *making* of lightning while Ps 136:5 and 7 are concerned with his prior *making* of the heavens and the great lights, respectively.

The third appearance of עשה ("make") in Ps 135 (v. 18) contrasts nicely with its other five occurrences in these two psalms. As with the three instances of the root עשה ("the one who makes") in Ps 136, it is a qal participle. Unlike the participles of Ps 136 whose subject is Yahweh, the subjects of this participle are the idol makers of the nations. This parallel distinguishes Yahweh not only from other gods but also from men. The מעשה ידי אדם ("work of human hands") in Ps 135:15 (another instance of the root עשה) are nothing more than lifeless idols (v. 17), but the works of Yahweh are great and wonderful (Ps 136:4). Yahweh makes/made lightning

---

9. The title אדון only occurs 13 times in the Psalter. Six of these appearances are in Book V, with half of these six occurring in Pss 135–136.

10. Although עשה is a common word, I have identified it as a key word because of its relationship to the major theme of these psalms (i.e., Yahweh's works separate him from other gods) and its rhetorically significant location in Ps 136:4.

Part 2: The Context of Psalms 135–137

(Ps 135:7), the heavens (Ps 136:5), the great lights (Ps 136:7), and does whatever he wants wherever he wants (Ps 135:6), but man's work results in an idol that cannot breathe (Ps 135:15–18).

Psalm 136:4, the theme-setting verse for the body of Ps 136, has important parallels with the theme-setting verse of Ps 135 (v. 5). First, the prepositional phrase לבדו ("to him alone") (Ps 136:4) accentuates Yahweh's matchlessness much like Ps 135:5 (גדול יהוה ואדנינו מכל־אלהים ["great is Yahweh and our Lord than all gods"]). Second, the adjective גדול ("great"), which describes the wonders of Yahweh in Ps 136:4, also appears in Ps 135:5. In this latter verse, Yahweh himself is גדול ("great"). Since Yahweh himself is great, one can only expect that his actions would be great.

In addition to its appearance in Ps 136:4, this adjective (גדול ["great"]) occurs two other times in Ps 136. First, it is used in Ps 136:7 to describe the lights that Yahweh made. Thus, the progression associated with Yahweh's greatness in Pss 135–136 can be sketched as follows: his being (Ps 135:5) → his actions in general (Ps 136:4) → his creation (Ps 136:7). The final instance of גדול ("great") in Ps 136 comes in v. 17. Here it does not describe Yahweh but the kings whom Yahweh struck. However great these kings may have been, Yahweh's victory over them demonstrates his superior greatness.

After their respective theme-setting verses, both psalms draw attention to Yahweh's work in relation to his creation. Lexically, the mention of השמים, הארץ, and המים ("the heavens," "the earth," and "the waters") in Ps 136:5–6 parallels Ps 135:6, which lists שמים, ארץ, ימים, and תהומות ("heavens," "earth," "seas," and "depths"),[11] and Ps 135:7, which references הארץ ("the earth"). The creation in Ps 135:6 serves as the arena in which Yahweh continually does what he pleases, while Ps 136:5–6 highlights Yahweh's original crafting of these various divisions of creation. This continuous vs. past perspective carries over into the subsequent verse(s) in each psalm. In Ps 135:7, the psalmist describes Yahweh's continuous work of producing clouds, lightning, and rain, but in Ps 136:7–9, the psalmist reflects on Yahweh's past construction of the great lights.

After dealing with Yahweh's works involving creation, both psalms give an overview of some of Yahweh's major historical acts, beginning with his slaughter of the Egyptian firstborn[12] and ending with his gift of land to

---

11. Both ימים and תהומות (Ps 135:6) parallel המים of Ps 136:5–6.

12. After their statements about Yahweh striking the Egyptian firstborn, the two psalms go in two different directions in their discussion of Egypt. Psalm 135 highlights the extent of the firstborn plague (v. 8) and references the other plagues by means of the phrase ומפתים אתות (v. 9). Psalm 136 focuses on Yahweh bringing Israel out (v. 11) and

Israel. These two sections are remarkably similar. First, the opening cola of Pss 136:10 and 135:8, in spite of their syntactical differences, are lexically and semantically the same.[13] Second, the only two references to Pharaoh in the Psalter are located in Pss 135:9 and 136:15, albeit in reference to two different events.[14] Third, the psalms's descriptions of Yahweh's defeat of other kings/nations and his subsequent gift of their land to Israel have the following similarities:[15] 1) both describe Yahweh's acts towards the kings/nations with the verbal word pair הרג/נכה (Ps 135:10; Ps 136:17–18);[16] 2) both have the verbal object מלכים (Ps 135:10; Ps 136:17–18), followed appositionally with the specifying phrase לסיחון מלך האמרי ולעוג מלך הבשן (Ps 135:11; Ps 136:19–20);[17] 3) with the exception of one syntactical difference (presence of the ל preposition before נחלה in Ps 136:21) and one lexical difference (Israel called עמו in Ps 135:12, but עבדו in Ps 136:22), the description of Yahweh's gift of the land is the same in both (Ps 135:12; Ps 136:21–22).

One of the key lexemes in these psalms' reviews of the plagues, exodus, and Red Sea crossing is תוך ("in the midst").[18] In Ps 135:9 this preposition denotes the location of Yahweh's plagues (בתוככי מצרים ["in the midst of Egypt"]). In Ps 136 it identifies Egypt as the place from which Israel was delivered (מתוכם ["from their midst"]) (v. 11) and the Red Sea as the place through which Israel passed (בתוכו ["in its midst"]) (v. 14). Because Yahweh sent his plagues "in the midst" of Egypt (Ps 135:9), Israel could be brought out "from the midst" of Egypt (Ps 136:11) and on their journey cross "in the midst" of the Red Sea (Ps 136:14).

---

the manner by which he did so (v. 12).

13. The same three roots (בכור, מצרים, נכה) describe Yahweh's striking of the Egyptian firstborn.

14. Psalm 135:9 mentions Pharaoh and his servants (עבדיו) as the objects of Yahweh's plagues, but Ps 136:15 names Pharaoh and his army (חילו) as the objects of Yahweh's toss into the Red Sea.

15. The major difference between these descriptions is the extent of conquest. Psalm 135 mentions the kingdoms of Canaan, but Ps 136 just mentions Sihon and Og. In addition, there are three lexical differences in these respective sections: 1) גוים and מלכים (Ps 135:10) vs. מלכים (x2) (Ps 136:17–18); 2) עצומים and רבים (Ps 135:10) vs. גדלים and אדירים (Ps 136:17–18); and 3) עמו (Ps 135:12) vs. עבדו (Ps 136:22).

16. This word pair (נכה/הרג) only appears in the Psalter in Ps 135:10 and 136:17–18.

17. These are the only two places in the Psalter where Sihon and Og are mentioned.

18. Howard (*Structure*, 100) identifies "most particles and many common words" as "incidental links." In Pss 135–136, תוך would be an exception because of its rhetorical significance in Ps 136, which I highlighted in my poetic analysis of that psalm.

Part 2: The Context of Psalms 135–137

The numerous parallels between the historical sections of these two psalms force the attentive reader to notice key differences. First, Ps 135 focuses solely on the beginning (Egypt) and end (Canaan) of Israel's journey, while Ps 136 includes significant events during the journey from Egypt to Canaan (i.e., the Red Sea and the wilderness). Second, the extent of Israel's journey is different in both psalms. Psalm 135 includes the kingdoms of Canaan (v. 11), a detail conspicuously absent from Ps 136, which, like the Pentateuch, stops with the kings on the east of the Jordan.[19] Third, Ps 135 deals almost exclusively with Yahweh's actions against kings/nations (i.e., Pharaoh/Egypt and kings/kingdoms on east and west sides of Jordan), but Ps 136 focuses more on Yahweh's care for Israel (i.e., the exodus, crossing of Red Sea, guidance in wilderness).[20] There is no doubt that Ps 136 also refers to Yahweh's actions against kings/kingdoms, but it always relates back to his people Israel (in contrast to Ps 135). Therefore, Ps 135 highlights Yahweh's relationship with Israel more in terms of election (v. 4) and general care (v. 14); in contrast, Ps 136 describes this relationship primarily in terms of historical deliverance (vv. 10–24).

In addition to the similarities between the historical sections of both psalms, there are lexical parallels between the historical section of Ps 136 and other sections within Ps 135 (i.e., outside of vv. 6–12). The first of these parallels is associated with the lexeme יצא ("bring out").[21] In Ps 135:7, the psalmist employs this lexeme to describe Yahweh's act of bringing the wind out of its storehouses (מוצא־רוח מאוצרותיו ["who brings wind from its storehouses"]). In Ps 136:11, it describes Yahweh's deliverance of Israel from Egypt (ויוצא ישראל מתוכם ["and he brought Israel out from their midst"]). Once again, this ties together Yahweh's actions in creation and the redemption of his people.

Last, the use of the title עבדו ("his servant") in Ps 136:22 serves as an important link back to Ps 135, in which the noun עבד ("servant") appears three times. Psalm 135 contrasts the servants of Yahweh (vv. 1, 14) with the

---

19. This is one of the reasons why Macholz ("Psalm 136," 178) argues that Ps 136 was composed at a time when (only) the Pentateuch was considered canonical. The other two reasons he gives are: 1) the parallels between Ps 136:4–9 and Gen 1:6–10, 14–18 and 2) the description of Yahweh's action against Pharaoh and his army in Ps 136:15 is only found in Exod 14:27. In contrast, the inclusion of the Canaanite conquest in Ps 135 supports a later date for its composition.

20. Cf. Hossfeld and Zenger, *Psalms*, 500. The exception is the reference to the gift of the land, which is present in both psalms.

21. This verb occurs in the hiphil in both instances.

servants of Pharaoh (v. 9). The former are called upon to praise Yahweh (v. 1) for many reasons, two of which are his plagues against the latter (v. 9) and his compassion upon his own servants (v. 14). Psalm 136:22 adds to the interpretive line associated with this root. Calling Israel עבדו ("his servant") brings the reader back to the last occurrence of עבד ("servant") in Ps 135 (v. 14), which highlights Yahweh's compassion on his servants. Consequently, Yahweh's gift of the land to Israel serves as an example of his compassion upon them (Ps 135:14).

After the historical overview in both psalms, the subsequent sections begin with a rhetorically significant switch in person. Psalm 135 transitions from third person to second person (Ps 135:13–14) while Psalm 136 changes from third person to first person (Ps 136:23–24). These two sections (Ps 135:13–14; Ps 136:23–25) are connected on thematic and lexical levels. Lexically, they share the root זכר ("remember").[22] The psalmist confesses that Yahweh's remembrance is forever in Ps 135:13. In Ps 136:23 Yahweh remembers his people in their lowliness. Thematically, they both are concerned with Yahweh's care for his people. Psalm 135:14 highlights his general care for his people, and Ps 136:23–24 underscores his care for his people in difficult times their enemies bring upon them.[23] As such, the mention of adversaries in Ps 136:24 (ויפרקנו מצרינו ["and he snatched us from our adversaries"]) recalls the references to Pharaoh, the Egyptians, and the kings in Pss 135–136.

One of the distinctive features of Ps 136 is that it moves beyond Yahweh's present care for Israel to his care for all creatures in v. 25. While Ps 135 does not focus on his present care of all creatures, it does highlight his present control of the elements. Consequently, Ḥakham connects Yahweh's provision of food for all flesh (Ps 136:25) to his giving of rain (Ps 135:7).[24] The latter serves as the means by which Yahweh accomplishes the former.

Psalm 137 in Relation to the Twin Psalms 135–136

At first glance, Ps 137 appears to be wholly unrelated to its surrounding psalms, which has led Leuenberger to term it an "orphan."[25] Its opening

---

22. Hossfeld and Zenger (*Psalms*, 520) identify this word as "a central topos in Psalms 135–136."
23. Cf. Goulder, *Psalms of the Return*, 217–18.
24. Ḥakham, *Psalms 101–150*, 382.
25. Leuenberger, *Konzeptionen*, 321.

PART 2: THE CONTEXT OF PSALMS 135–137

reference to the people's exile in Babylon puts it well beyond the historical outlook of the previous two psalms. Its lamenting, determined, and vengeful tone contrasts with the celebratory, worshipful tone of Pss 135–136. Yet, its juxtaposition with these two psalms demands a closer inspection, upon which one quickly finds significant thematic and lexical parallels. For a list of these parallels, see tables 4 and 5 below.

Table 4. Thematic Parallels between Psalms 135–136 and 137

Psalms 135–136	Psalms 137
ויפרקנו (v. 24)	יאחז ונפץ (v. 9)
צרינו (v. 24)	תוללינו and שובינו (v. 3)
Defeat of Israel's Enemies	Victory of Israel's Enemies
Destruction of Firstborn (135:8; 136:10)	Judgment of Children (v. 9)
Possession of Land as Inheritance	Captivity in Foreign Land

Table 5. Lexical Parallels between Psalms 135–136 and 137

Psalms 135–136	Psalm 137
זכר (135:13; 136:23)	זכר (vv. 1, 6, 7)
ציון (135:21)	ציון (vv. 1, 3)
תוך (135:9; 136:11, 14)	תוך (v. 2)
יהוה (135:1, 2, 3, 5, 6, 13, 14, 19, 20, 21; 136:1)	יהוה (vv. 4, 7)
ירושלם (135:21)	ירושלם (vv. 5, 6, 7)
עלה (135:7)	עלה (v. 6)
יום (136:8)	יום (v. 7)

In my poetic analysis of Ps 136, I noted that vv. 23–24 are distinct because of their 1p references. Interestingly, most of the parallels between Pss 136 and 137 revolve around these two verses, indicating that Ps 137 stands as a response to the affirmations of Ps 136:23–24. The first parallel between Ps 137 and these two verses is the dominance of the 1p perspective. While vv. 23–24 are the only two 1p verses in Ps 136, Ps 137 is written almost exclusively in the first person.[26] Could this be simple coincidence, or is this part of the editorial significance of the juxtaposition of these two psalms?

26. Cf. Leuenberger, *Konzeptionen*, 321. The first and last stanzas are in the 1P, but the middle stanza is in the 1S.

Contextual Analysis of the Psalm Group 135–137

The purpose of this connection may be to identify the exiles of Ps 137 with the worshippers of Ps 136.

The second link between Ps 137 and Ps 136:23–24 is the repetition of the root זכר ("remember").[27] In the poetic analysis of Ps 137, I noted the prevalence and significance of this root. It appears in every stanza of Ps 137 and its antonym שׁכח ("forget") is present in the middle stanza. Of these instances of זכר ("remember"), the command to Yahweh in Ps 137:7 intersects most clearly with Ps 136:23–24. The psalmist's command that Yahweh *remember* the Edomites for what they did to Jerusalem is a direct response to the affirmation of Ps 136:23 that Yahweh *remembered* his people in their low estate. In other words, the psalmist is asking Yahweh to do exactly what Ps 136:23 affirms he had done in the past.

The further explication of Ps 136:24 strengthens this interpretation. In this verse, the cause of the people's lowliness is their enemies; conversely, Yahweh's remembrance involves snatching his people from their enemies. The specific mention of Edom and Babylon in Ps 137 as the objects of Yahweh's remembrance demonstrates that the imperative of Ps 137:7 may well have been a response to the affirmation of Ps 136:23–24. The people are praying for Yahweh to act against these latter enemies just as he had acted against their earlier enemies (Pss 135–136). Furthermore, this may explain one of the key differences between Pss 135 and 136. The emphasis of Ps 136 on Yahweh's deliverance of his people from their enemies (in contrast to Ps 135; see above) sets the reader up for the situation in Ps 137 and proves to be a basis for the prayer against Israel's enemies in Ps 137:7–9.

The parallels involving זכר ("remember") in relation to Ps 136:23–24 are not limited to Ps 137:7. One may also interpret the first occurrence of זכר ("remember") in Ps 137 (v. 1) in light of Ps 136:23. In the former, the people's remembrance of Zion was the cause of their weeping, but in the latter Yahweh's remembrance of his people was the impetus behind his rescue of them.

The psalmist's oath to remember (זכר) Jerusalem in vv. 5–6 also links back to Ps 136:23 and even Ps 135:1–5. The psalmist defines his remembrance of Jerusalem in v. 6cd as making Jerusalem his highest joy. The reference to Yahweh's remembrance of his people in Ps 136:23 also carries connotations of deep affections toward his people. The only two 1cp references of Ps 135 (vv. 1 & 5) confirm this connotation. Here, the psalmist refers to Yahweh as אלהינו ("our God") (v. 1) and אדנינו ("our Lord") (v. 5).

---

27. Cf. Hossfeld and Zenger, *Psalms*, 520–1.

Part 2: The Context of Psalms 135–137

In between these two titles for Yahweh, the psalmist states that Yahweh had chosen Israel for סגלתו ("his possession"). The result of these connections is that Yahweh remembers his people (Ps 136:23) because of their special place in his affections (Ps 135:1–5). In like manner, the psalmist's remembrance of Jerusalem means that Jerusalem must be first in his affections. Therefore, the psalmist's memory of Jerusalem is akin to Yahweh's remembrance of his people.

In this same vein, there are also two thematic parallels between Ps 136:23–24 and Ps 137. First, Ps 136:24 uses the verb פרק to describe Yahweh's deliverance of his people from their enemies. This verb often carries connotations of "tearing apart or off."[28] Thus, this action involves a grasping of the object with one's hands, often with aggression. If such is the meaning in Ps 136:24, then God's rescue of Israel is portrayed anthropomorphically. God tears/snatches his people from the clutches of their enemies. Such an idea is also found in Ps 137:9. Here, the people pronounce a blessing on the one who grasps and shatters the children of Babylon on a rock. The first verb אחז ("grasp") is similar to פרק ("snatch away") in that both involve the act of grabbing. The former is certainly more neutral than the latter; thus, their meanings have very little semantic overlap. However, the rest of Ps 137:9 definitely gives an aggressive or violent flavor to the verse. Therefore, Yahweh's snatching of his people from their enemies in Ps 136:24 parallels Ps 137:9 where the people bless the one who snatches and smashes the Babylonian children. In both instances, Yahweh's remembrance involves someone falling into his clutches. Thus, as was evident in Pss 135–136, Yahweh's deliverance of his people usually involves a violent action against their opponents.

The second thematic parallel between Ps 137 and Ps 136:23–24 relates to the designations of their enemies. Psalm 137:3 uses two terms for the Babylonians: 1) שובינו ("our captors") and 2) תוללינו ("our tormentors"). As previously noted, the second designation makes it unmistakably clear that cordiality towards Israel was not one of the Babylonian's best qualities. The term צרינו ("our adversaries") in Ps 136:24 is related to these two terms since the reference to the Babylonians as captors (137:3) identifies them as one of Israel's enemies (136:24).

Parallels related to the memory motif in Ps 137 are not limited to Ps 136:23–24 but extend to other verses in Pss 135–136. For example, the emphasis on Yahweh's remembrance in Ps 137:7 echoes his eternalm

---

28. See BDB, 830 and HALOT, 3:975.

Contextual Analysis of the Psalm Group 135–137

remembrance in Ps 135:13 (יהוה זכרך לדר־ודר ["O Yahweh, your remembrance is from generation to generation"]).[29] Psalm 135:14 connects his eternal renown to his vindication of and compassion on his people. The cry in Ps 137:7–9 is therefore not only a cry for deliverance, but read in light of Ps 135:13–14, a cry for Yahweh to uphold his reputation as the one who vindicates his people.

On the thematic level, there are two major contrasts between Pss 135–136 and Ps 137. One of the key themes in Pss 135–136 is Yahweh's defeat of Israel's enemies. Both psalms rehearse Yahweh's defeat of Pharaoh, Sihon, and Og, with Ps 135 adding the kingdoms of Canaan. By opening Ps 137 with the setting of exile and captivity, the reader encounters a strong contrast and is drawn back to Israel's earlier position in Egypt, which is highlighted in Ps 136:11–12. Lexically, this connection is made by means of the parallel phrases בתוכה ("in its midst") (Ps 137:2) and מתוכם ("from their midst") (Ps 136:11). Just as the people had been captives in Egypt (Ps 136:11), so Ps 137 opens with their captivity in Babylon. It then comes as no surprise that Ps 137 concludes with a prayer for judgment on their enemies (vv. 7–9). Although the people were probably no longer been in Babylon,[30] they still await Yahweh's judgment of their enemies, Edom and Babylon, just as he had judged the Egyptians.[31]

The type of judgment outlined in Ps 137:8–9 and Ps 136:11–12 confirms a connection between these passages. Psalms 135:8 and 136:10 both describe Yahweh's striking of the Egyptian firstborn (בכור). In Ps 137:9 the psalmist specifies the extent of vengeance he desires Babylon to experience, namely, he wants the judgment to include their children (עלליך). Hence, the people's request for Babylon's judgment in Ps 137:9 goes beyond Yahweh's judgment of Egypt. They did not simply request the destruction of the firstborn (as in Egypt), but the destruction of all the children in Babylon.

The second thematic contrast revolves around the land.[32] The numerous topographical references in the first four verses of Ps 137 create a major

---

29. Hossfeld and Zenger (*Psalms*, 521) write of this link: "But the 'memory of Zion' invoked in Ps 137:1b, 6b also acheives a further dimension within the horizon of Ps 135:13: 'memory, remembering' is the medium given, or assigned, to Israel in Exod 3:15 by Yhwh himself for preserving its origin and its collective identity 'from generation to generation.'"

30. For a discussion of the date of writing of Ps 137 date of writing, see my above analysis of Ps 137.

31. Hossfeld and Zenger, *Psalms*, 521.

32. Ballhorn, *Zum Telos*, 261.

Part 2: The Context of Psalms 135–137

disparity when read in light of the two previous psalms.³³ Psalms 135–136 end their historical overview with the affirmation that God gave Israel their enemies' land as an inheritance. In Ps 137 the people recall their time in their enemies' land not as victors (Pss 135–136) but as captives (Ps 137).³⁴ Specifically, the description of Babylon as אדמת נכר ("foreign soil") (Ps 137:4) contrasts with the land of promise that is described four times in Pss 135–136 as נחלה ("inheritance") (Pss 135:12; 136:21–22).

So far, every parallel highlighted in this section in some way relates to Ps 136. However, the two Zion references in Ps 137 (vv. 1 and 3) find no parallel in Ps 136, but correspond to the final verse of Ps 135, where the psalmist affirms that Yahweh is blessed from Zion (v. 21). In contrast to this latter verse, the people's position in Babylon made it impossible for them to bless Yahweh from Zion (Ps 135:21).³⁵ Instead of praise for Yahweh going out from Zion to the peoples of the world,³⁶ the people of Zion had been asked to sing Yahweh songs in a foreign land (Ps 137:3).

In summary, Ps 137 draws on two of the major themes of Pss 135–136. First, in response to Yahweh's deliverance of Israel by means of his judgment of their enemies, Ps 137 recalls their captivity in Babylon and petitions Yahweh to judge both Babylon and Edom, the two pre-eminent enemies of Israel. Second, the recollection of the people's time in Babylon contrasts with the land that Yahweh gave them as an inheritance in Pss 135–136.

In addition to these two themes, Ps 137 responds directly to the affirmation of Ps 136:23–24 that Yahweh remembered his people when they were in a lowly state (i.e., he delivered them from their enemies). Although Ps 137 does not request deliverance for the people, it does request that Yahweh remember his people's enemies. Regardless of Israel's location,³⁷ it is apparent that they have not experienced their full deliverance because Yahweh has yet to "remember" their enemies.

---

33. Allen, *Psalms 101–150*, 307.

34. See Hossfeld and Zenger, *Psalms*, 509.

35 Hossfeld and Zenger (*Psalms*, 521) write, "Psalm 137 then consitutes, in a sense retroactively . . . , a dramatic *Sitz im Leben* for the psalms composition Psalms 120–134, 135–136. That composition now stands within the dialectic of suffering and joy sung in Psalm 137, as well as in the dialectic of Yhwh's apparent impotence in the face of enemies threatening Zion and Yhwh's omnipotence."

36. Ibid.

37. If Ps 137 is a post-exilic psalm, then some of the people are back in the land of Israel.

5

Psalms 135–137 in the Context of Book V

The next step in determining the contextual function of Pss 135–137 is to direct our attention to the two major psalm groups that bracket these three psalms. For this reason, we now turn out attention first to the relationship between Pss 135–137 and the Songs of Ascents and then the Last Davidic Psalter. After we have examined the relationship between these three psalm groups, we will consider the role of Pss 135–137 in the structure of Book V at the conclusion of this chapter.

PSALMS 135–137 IN RELATION TO THE SONGS OF ASCENTS

The collection of psalms (Pss 120–134) immediately preceding Pss 135–137 has been termed the "Songs of Ascents," a common translation of their shared superscription (שיר המעלות). In addition to their common superscription, they are united by their similar length, lexical features, and motifs.[1] The purpose of the following investigation is to determine how Pss 135–137 relate to this psalm group. This discussion consists of three major sections: 1) Connections at the Seam: Psalm 135 and Psalms 133–134, 2)

---

1. See Ḥakham, *Psalms 101–150*, 365ff.; Crow, *Songs of Ascents*, 129; and Ballhorn, *Zum Telos*, 251. Grossberg (*Centripetal and Centrifugal Structures*, 17) emphasizes "that of all the psalms with headings in the Psalter, it is only the Songs of Ascents which appear consecutively—no Song of Ascents appears in the MT outside of this small collection."

Part 2: The Context of Psalms 135–137

Major Themes and Their Echoes in Psalms 135–137, and 3) Psalm 132: Its Importance and Relationship to Psalms 135–137.

Connections at the Seam: Psalm 135 and Psalms 133–134

To say that Ps 135 has strong ties with the last couple of psalms in the Songs of Ascents is an understatement. The lexical repetitions between Pss 134 and 135 are some of the most obvious repetitions in the Psalter. Excluding the superscript (שיר המעלות), 14 of the 23 words of Ps 134 reappear in Ps 135 (61 percent).[2] These lexical repetitions are not simply random but are repetitions of entire phrases at the beginning, middle, and end of Ps 135. See table 6 below for a list of these parallels.

Table 6. Lexical Parallels between Psalms 134 and 135

Psalm 134	Psalm 135
ברכו את־יהוה (vv. 1–2)	ברכו את־יהוה (vv. 19–20)
עבדי יהוה (v. 1)	עבדי יהוה (v. 1)
העמדים בבית־יהוה (v. 1)	שעמדים בבית יהוה (v. 2)
יברכך יהוה מציון (v. 3)	ברוך יהוה מציון (v. 21)
עשה שמים וארץ (v. 3)	יהוה עשה בשמים ובארץ (v. 6)

The twice given command ברכו את־יהוה ("bless Yahweh") of Ps 134 (vv. 1–2) is repeated four times at the end of Ps 135 (vv. 19–20), where it serves as the second half of the psalm's frame (the first half being vv. 1–4). Those commanded to bless Yahweh in Ps 134:1 (כל־עבדי יהוה ["all the servants of Yahweh"]) and the descriptive phrase that specifies their location (העמדים בבית־יהוה בלילות ["who stand in the house of Yahweh at night"]) (v. 1) also appear in Psalm 135 with a few slight alterations.[3]

---

2. The brevity of Ps 134 is one factor that made such repetition possible. With only 23 words, an editor could easily replicate many of these words in a psalm the length of Ps 135 (21 verses).

3. First, these two phrases do not appear at the end of Ps 135 with the fourfold command to bless Yahweh, but with the command הללו את־שם יהוה at the beginning of Ps 135. Second, the lexeme כל is omitted in Ps 135:1b, and the relative pronoun ש (instead of the definite article as in Ps 134:1) is prefixed to the participle עמדים in Ps 135:2a. Last, the locative adverbial phrase בחצרות בית אלהינו in Ps 135:2b replaces the prepositional phrase בלילות (Ps 134:1).

Psalms 135–137 in the Context of Book V

The only alteration that appears theologically motivated is the use of the locative adverbial phrase בחצרות בית אלהינו ("in the courts of the house of our God") in Ps 135:2b instead of the prepositional phrase בלילות ("in the night") (Ps 134:1). Its significance becomes evident when one considers the only other mention of the courts of Yahweh's house in Book V. In Ps 116, the psalmist states twice נדרי ליהוה אשלם נגדה־נא לכל־עמו ("I will repay my vows to Yahweh before all his people") (vv. 14, 18). After the second instance, the psalmist gives a further clarification: בחצרות בית יהוה בתוככי ירושלם ("in the courts of the house of Yahweh in the midst of you, O Jerusalem") (v. 19). As a result of the juxtaposition of Ps 116:18, 19, one can conclude that the courts are the location of the entirety of Yahweh's people. Thus, the difference between Pss 134:1 and 135:2 is a broadening of the referents of עבדי יהוה ("servants of Yahweh").[4] The use of בלילות ("in the night") in Ps 134 restricts the referents to the priests or Levites,[5] but the phrase בחצרות בית אלהינו ("in the courts of the house of our God") in Ps 135 broadens the referents to all of Yahweh's people.[6] Such an expansion accords well with the mention of יראי יהוה ("Yahweh fearers") at the end of Ps 135 (v. 20).

Both phrases in Ps 134:3 reappear in Ps 135 with slight modifications. The phrase יברכך יהוה מציון ("Yahweh bless you from Zion") (v. 3a) recurs in Ps 135:21. In this latter verse, the verb becomes a passive participle and the 2ms pronominal suffix disappears. So, instead of Yahweh *blessing* from Zion, he *is blessed* from Zion. This switch reinforces the commands of the psalm's frame (vv. 1–4; 19–20) for all his people to praise and bless him. As he blesses his people, their appropriate response is to bless him from Zion.

The second phrase (עשה שמים וארץ) ("maker of heaven and earth") in Ps 134:3 appears in Ps 135:6 with a couple of changes.[7] Because of these changes, the two verses differ on the semantic level. Psalm 134:3 affirms Yahweh as the maker of the heavens and the earth, whereas Ps 135:6 stresses Yahweh's ability to act according to his pleasure in the heavens and

---

4. Eaton (*Psalms*, 296) and Hossfeld and Zenger (*Psalms*, 496–97) each connect this phrase to Ps 113:1 wherein is a similar call to worship. Hossfeld and Zenger argue that the universal portrait of Ps 113:2–3 indicates that these servants are from all the peoples of the world.

5. Contra Goldingay, *Psalms 90–150*, 578.

6. Hossfeld and Zenger (*Psalms*, 497) connect Ps 135:1–2 to Ps 100:4, where all the earth is invited to come into the courts of Yahweh with praise.

7. First, a ב preposition appears before both of the objects (וארץ שמים). Second, the qal participle of Ps 134:3 is changed to a qal perfect.

the earth (i.e., the realm of his creation). The latter builds on the former since Yahweh as Creator is a prerequisite for Yahweh's freedom to act freely within his creation.

Because Ps 133 contains language and imagery similar to Ps 134, it is important to investigate how this psalm might function at the seam between these two groups. Even though the parallels are not as extensive, Ps 135 exhibits associations with Ps 133 (see table 7 below for a list of these parallels). The most important parallel is the reference to Zion in Ps 133:3, and in particular, the supplemental information given about Zion. After identifying Zion as the place where Yahweh commanded his blessing, the appositional phrase חיים עד־העולם ("life forevermore") clarifies the blessing. This eternal life parallels the emphasis in the center of Ps 135 on the Lord's own eternality (v. 13). Thus, Yahweh's own eternal existence undergirds his blessing of eternal life.

Table 7. Lexical Parallels between Psalms 133 and 135

Psalm 133	Psalm 135
נעים/טוב (v. 1)^A	נעים/טוב (v. 3)
זקן־אהרן (v. 2)	בית אהרן (v. 19)
ציון (v. 3)	ציון (v. 21)
הברכה (v. 3)	ברכו (vv. 19–20); ברוך (v. 21)
עד־העולם (v. 3)	לעולם (v. 13)

   A. Outside of these two psalms, this word pair only occurs in one other place in the Psalter: 147:1.

Major Themes and Their Echoes in Psalms 135–137

There are several ways that one could adduce the intertextual relationships between Pss 135–137 and the Songs of Ascents. Since one can best summarize the primary message of the Songs by tracing its major themes, the subsequent discussion consists of an overview of these themes with an eye toward their reverberations in Pss 135–137.

Psalms 135–137 in the Context of Book V

Yahweh as the Maker of Heaven and Earth

One of the key phrases within the Songs of Ascents is the description of the Lord as the עשה שמים וארץ ("maker of heaven and earth"), appearing three times across this collection of psalms (Pss 121:2; 124:8; 134:3).[8] The first two occurrences of this phrase are associated with the notion that Yahweh is the people's helper (עזר).[9] Thus, Yahweh's making of the heaven and the earth undergirds his people's confidence in his ability to help them.

The emphasis on Yahweh as maker of the heaven and earth is also an important theme in Pss 135–136. In particular, Ps 136 highlights his creation of the heaven and earth as a reason for his people to give him praise (vv. 5–9). Psalm 135, on the other hand, focuses on his ongoing ability to act in his creation (v. 6), using the same lexemes (ארץ, שמים, עשה ["make," "heaven," "earth"]) as the phrase in the Songs of Ascents. In both psalms, his work of/in creation is followed by a rehearsal of his acts of deliverance for his people, much like the phrase עשה שמים וארץ ("maker of heaven and earth") in the Songs of Ascents is linked to Yahweh as the helper of his people (Ps 121:2; Ps 124:8).

The Peace of Jerusalem/Israel

A second theme throughout the Songs of Ascents is the peace of Jerusalem/Israel. Although the first hint of this theme appears in Ps 121 where the psalmist describes Yahweh as שומר ישראל ("he who guards Israel") (v. 4), the theme finds its preeminent expression in Ps 122. In this psalm an individual celebrates the gathering of the tribes together in Jerusalem (vv. 1–5) and exhorts others to join him in seeking the peace of Jerusalem (vv. 6–9).[10] This petition for the peace of Jerusalem indicates that the euphoria recounted in vv. 1–5 is absent at the time of the psalm's writing.

The psalmist links the peace of Jerusalem to the rule of the Davidic dynasty by highlighting the Davidic house in v. 5 (כי שמה ישבו כסאות למשפט

---

8. Crow (*Songs of Ascents*, 138) notes only two other occurrences of this phrase in the Psalter: Pss 115:15 and 146:6 (both in Book V). Closely related to this epithet for Yahweh is the description of him as הישבי בשמים in Ps 123:1. Such a portrayal reappears in Ps 136:26, where Yahweh is אל השמים.

9. In Ps 121:2, the psalmist affirms עזרי מעם יהוה. In Ps 124:8, the acknowledgement is in the plural: עזרנו בשם יהוה.

10. The emphasis on peace in this psalm recalls the individual of Ps 120 who (in contrast to his enemies) pursues peace (vv. 6–7).

PART 2: THE CONTEXT OF PSALMS 135–137

כסאות לבית דויד ["for there thrones sat for judgment, thrones for the house of David"]). Such a connection is significant since the key psalm of this group (Ps 132) deals specifically with Yahweh's fulfillment of the Davidic Covenant.[11] Hence, the Jerusalemites will experience complete peace when the ultimate Davidic king is upon the throne of David.[12]

Outside of Ps 122, there are two other requests for the peace of Israel in the Songs of Ascents. In both instances, this petition is located at the end of a psalm that outlines the blessings that come upon those who trust in (Ps 125)/fear (Ps 128) Yahweh. Psalm 125 describes Yahweh's protection of his people/the righteous (vv. 1–3) and concludes with a prayer for Yahweh to bless those who are good and to judge the wicked (vv. 4–5). The reference to the peace of Israel at the end of v. 5 indicates that the peace of Israel is one of the blessings that Yahweh bestows upon his people (v. 2) who trust in him (v. 1) and are righteous (v. 3)/good (v. 4).

In like manner, Ps 128 reflects on the blessings of those who fear Yahweh.[13] The blessings described in this psalm are twofold: 1) blessing upon the man's household (vv. 2, 3, 6a)[14] and 2) the good of Jerusalem (v. 5). Once again, the request for the peace of Israel (v. 6b) is attached to a description of the blessings on those who follow Yahweh. Thus, two of the many blessings Yahweh-fearers receive are the good of Jerusalem (v. 5) and the peace of Israel (v. 6).

The opening verses of Pss 135–136 are very similar to the opening verses of Ps 122.[15] This parallel connects the future peace of Israel (Ps 122)

---

11. Crow (*Songs of Ascents*, 145) also makes this connection: "Also like Psalm 132, Psalm 122 offers a nostalgic view of the kingship of David as a reason for desiring and praying for Jerusalem's good."

12. The presence of שׁ in Ps 122:4 may indicate that the psalmist is recounting the past. (cf. Crow, *Songs of Ascents*, 46).

13. While the blessing of Yahweh is another key theme in the Songs of Ascents, I do not discuss it as a separate theme because Yahweh's blessing is related to Zion in every instance except one: Ps 128:5. See Ballhorn (*Zum Telos*, 251), who writes, "It is always emphasized that every blessing emanates from Zion." (Author's translation of "Es wird immer wieder betont, daß jeder Segen vom Zion ausgeht.")

14. These household blessings are also a key component of Ps 127:3–5, which focuses on the blessing of sons.

15. Psalms 122 and 135 share the following lexemes: בית יהוה (Ps 122:1; Ps 135:2), עמד (Ps 122:2; Ps 135:2), יה (Ps 122:4; Ps 135:4), and ישראל (Ps 122:4; Ps 135:4). There is also a key link between Ps 122:4 (להדות לשם יהוה) and Ps 136:1–3, 26 (the inclusio which calls for the thanksgiving of Yahweh) since both focus on the praise of Yahweh in his house.

with Yahweh's preexilic victories over Israel's enemies (Pss 135–136). Thus, in order to achieve the ultimate peace of Israel, Yahweh must act against Israel's later (eschatological?) enemies just as he had acted against their earlier enemies.

The emphasis on the peace of Jerusalem/Israel in the Songs of Ascents finds a shocking contrast in Ps 137. Such a contrast is highlighted by two key lexical connections between Pss 122 and 137. First, when invited to go to the house of the Lord, the psalmist affirms his gladness (שׂמחתי) in Ps 122:1. Such gladness is not only absent from Ps 137 but the captors' request for such gladness (שׂמחה) brings great grief to the captives (v. 3). The second lexical connection is closely related. After remembering the joy of being in the midst of Jerusalem, the psalmist petitions his readers in Ps 122:6: שׁאלו שׁלום ירושׁלם ("ask for the peace of Jerusalem"). In Ps 137:3 the captors demand songs of joy from the inhabitants of Jerusalem (כי שׁם שׁאלונו שׁובינו דברי־שׁיר ["for there our captors asked us for words of a song"]).[16] Such a parallel enhances the taunting nature of the Babylonian's request in Ps 137.

The connection between the fear of/trust in Yahweh and the peace of Israel in Pss 125 and 128 adds a new dimension to Ps 137. The obvious lack of peace in Israel reflected in Ps 137 implies that the people had not feared/trusted in Yahweh, a concept (exile as the result of rebellion) made explicit in the opening psalm of Book V (Ps 107).[17] To use the words of Ps 125, Israel did not receive good things from the Lord because they were not good (v. 4), but instead, יוליכם יהוה את־פעלי האון ("Yahweh causes them to walk with the workers of iniquity") (v. 5). As will be noted below, the only solution for this problem is for Yahweh to redeem them from their sins (Ps 130:7–8).

The Suffering of Israel and Yahweh's Deliverance of His People

Intermingled among the requests for the peace of Jerusalem/Israel is another theme, viz., the suffering of Israel at the hand of others. As soon as one leaves the peace-laden Ps 122, Ps 123 indicates that such peace is missing at this point in the Psalter. In this psalm, the people look expectantly to Yahweh for mercy as they are dealing with the contempt (vv. 3–4) of those who are proud and at ease (v. 4). In a similar manner, the psalmist in Ps 129 calls on Israel to remember how Yahweh had helped them in all their

---

16. The root שׁאל only occurs three times in Book V: Pss 109:10, 122:6, and 137:3.
17. See especially Ps 107:11, 17.

Part 2: The Context of Psalms 135–137

afflictions from youth (vv. 1–4) and prays for Yahweh to judge those who hate Zion (vv. 5–8).

In conjunction with the suffering of Israel, this psalm group also recalls Yahweh's rescue of Israel in these times of distress. For example, Ps 124 underscores Yahweh's protection of Israel when men rose up against them. Because of his protection, Yahweh should be blessed (v. 6). Also, Ps 126 recounts the joy of the people at their return from captivity (vv. 1–3). Nevertheless, the psalmist petitions Yahweh to return the captivity (v. 4), indicating the expectation of a more extensive return (כאפיקים בנגב ["as the rivers in the Negev"]).

Psalms 130–131—two psalms in which the psalmist serves as an example for Israel[18]—outline the appropriate response for Israel in their distress. Both psalms exhort Israel in the following manner: יחל ישראל אל־יהוה ("O Israel, hope in Yahweh"). In Ps 130:7–8, this exhortation is anchored in Yahweh's loving-kindness and future redemption of Israel from their sins.[19] In Ps 131:3, the extent of their hope is forever. Appropriately, these two psalms are immediately followed by Ps 132 and its hope in the Davidic Covenant.[20] Thus, their hopes will be fulfilled when this covenant finds its complete fulfillment.

The theme of Israel's suffering and Yahweh's deliverance dominates Pss 135–137. Psalm 135, wherein the psalmist commands Yahweh's servants to praise Yahweh (v. 1), their Lord (v. 5) who has compassion on his servants (v. 14), echoes the comparison in Ps 123 of Israel's dependence on Yahweh to servants looking to their masters. The blessing of Yahweh (ברוך יהוה ["blessed be Yahweh"]) for deliverance in Ps 124:6 reappears at the end of Ps 135 (v. 21), wherein similar deliverances are recounted (vv. 8–14).[21]

The joy that accompanies the return from captivity in Ps 126 (vv. 2, 3, 5, 6) contrasts with the absence of such joy in Ps 137 (vv. 1–4). In a similar manner, the description of weeping in Ps 137:1–2 is reminiscent

---

18. Crow, *Songs of Ascents*, 142.

19. This mention of the need for redemption from sins supports the earlier interpretation of the relationship between Pss 125, 128, and 137.

20. Allen (*Psalms 101–150*, 76) states concerning this connection: "[T]he eschatological function [of Psalm 132] receives a preliminary fanfare in the form of calls to Israel to . . . 'hope in Yahweh.'"

21. The metaphorical description of Yahweh's protection of his people in Ps 124:6 (שלא נתננו טרף לשניהם) has some interesting parallels to Psalms 135–136. In these latter psalms, Yahweh did not give his people as prey to their enemies, but he gave (נתן) their enemies' land to them as an inheritance (Pss 135:12 and 136:21).

Psalms 135–137 in the Context of Book V

of the phrase הזרעים בדמעה ("those who sow in tears") in Ps 126:5. Such a parallel produces hope that the joyful reaping of Ps 126:5 will one day be realized. Also, the double affirmation of Yahweh's acts of greatness in Ps 126 (by the nations in v. 2 and by the "captives of Zion" in v. 3) parallels the similar emphasis in Pss 135–136. In both, his ability to do great things (136:4)—both in his creation and in his deeds toward his people—validates his superiority over all other gods (Ps 135:5).

Furthermore, several themes from Ps 129 echo across Pss 135–137. The affirmation that Israel had been oppressed from their youth (vv. 1–2) parallels Pss 135–137 in several ways. First, Pss 135–136 outline this history of oppression when the psalmist(s) recounts Yahweh's past rescues of his people from their oppressors. Second, the noun form of the verb that describes this oppression (צרר in vv. 1–2) appears in Ps 136:24 (ויפרקנו מצרינו ["and he snatched us from our adversaries"]), thus emphasizing that Yahweh has been faithful to deliver his people from oppression throughout their history. In addition, the prayer against כל שנאי ציון ("all who hate Zion") in Ps 129:5–8 is given specificity and emphasis in Ps 137:7–9, where blessing is not only withheld from these Zion-haters (129:8), but is given to the one who executes judgment on them (137:8–9).

Finally, the reasons given for Israel to hope in Yahweh (Pss 130–131) are key connections to Pss 135–136. In Ps 130:7 the command is anchored in Yahweh's חסד ("loving-kindness"), the attribute to which all of Yahweh's actions relate in Ps 136. In Ps 131:3, the psalmist commands Israel to hope in the Lord מעתה ועד־עולם ("from now until forever").[22] The only reason such a hope is possible is because Yahweh's שם ("name") (Ps 135:13) and חסד ("loving-kindness") (refrain of Ps 136) are לעולם ("to forever").

Zion

The last theme of the Songs of Ascents is Zion.[23] Outside of the first two references to Zion in the Songs (Ps 125:1; 126:1), the remaining references highlight Yahweh's choice of Zion and his blessing of/from Zion. Earlier in the discussion of Ps 128, I noted how Yahweh's blessing of his fearers

---

22. This command to hope in Yahweh forever echoes similar language used earlier in the Songs of Ascents (Pss 121:8; 125:2).

23. Ballhorn (*Zum Telos*, 251) states, "The Zion theology forms the center around which the psalms [of Ascents] circle." (Author's translation of "Die Zionstheologie bildet die Mitte, um die die Psalmen kreisen.")

Part 2: The Context of Psalms 135–137

includes the goodness of Jerusalem and the peace of Israel. In v. 5 of this psalm, Yahweh's blessing is connected to Zion when the psalmist states: יברכך יהוה מציון ("Yahweh bless you from Zion").[24]

In the next psalm (Ps 129), Zion and blessing again connect, but in a manner quite different from their connection in Ps 128:5. In this psalm the psalmist prays against כל שנאי ציון ("all who hate Zion") (v. 5). Among other things, the psalmist predicts a withholding of blessing from these Zion-haters: ולא אמרו העברים ברכת־יהוה אליכם ברכנו אתכם בשם יהוה ("Those who pass by will not say 'May Yahweh's blessing be yours. We bless you in the name of Yahweh.'") (v. 8). Since they hate Zion, the psalmist sees no need for them to receive the blessing of Yahweh that comes from Zion (Ps 128:5).

Psalm 132 contains the most extensive description of Zion in the Songs of Ascents. As Yahweh's choice for his eternal dwelling place (vv. 13–14), the psalmist describes the many blessings that will come upon Zion. These blessings (ברך in v. 15) include provision (v. 15), provision for the poor (v. 15), salvation of her priests (v. 16), joy for her saints (v. 16), and the Davidic throne (vv. 17–18).[25] Specifically, Yahweh's blessings related to the Davidic throne are the exaltation of his anointed (v. 17) and the judgment of his enemies (v. 18).

In the next psalm (Ps 133), the psalmist again identifies Zion as the place of Yahweh's blessing (v. 3), yet defines the blessing as חיים עד־העולם ("life forevermore") (v. 3). Such eternal language parallels the designation of Zion as Yahweh's eternal dwelling place (132:14) and the affirmation of the eternal existence of Zion (125:1). The last verse of the Songs of Ascents (Ps 134:3)—which repeats Ps 128:5 (יברכך יהוה מציון ["Yahweh bless you from Zion"])—contrains the final mention of Zion in the psalm group, thus preparing the reader for the continued Zion conversation of Pss 135–137.

Zion's presence in Pss 135–137 is limited to the first and last psalms in this group. The only mention of Zion in Ps 135 comes in the final verse where Yahweh is blessed from Zion (v. 21). When one turns to Ps 137, the captives' remembrance of Zion is the source of their grief (vv. 1–2), especially when their mockers ask them to sing "songs of Zion" (v. 3–4).[26] Psalm

---

24. Crow (*Songs of Ascents*, 137) highlights the parallels between this idea and Pss 14:7/53:7 and Isa 2:1–4/Mic 4:1–4.

25. According to Brennan, ("Hidden Harmonies," 141) the key question is: "[W]ill he not also restore the Davidic monarchy, according to his promise (vv. 11–12, 17–18)?"

26. Ballhorn, *Zum Telos*, 261.

Psalms 135–137 in the Context of Book V

137 therefore indicates that the people have not experienced the ultimate blessing of Zion (as spoken of in Ps 132:13–18) because Yahweh has yet to judge Israel's enemies (vv. 7–9).

Psalm 132: Its Importance and Relationship to Psalms 135–137

A simple perusal of the Songs of Ascents reveals the disparity of the length of Psalm 132 in comparison to the other Songs. With its eighteen verses, it is double the size of the next longest psalm (Ps 122) and is six times longer than the shortest psalms (Pss 133, 134). Yet its distinction does not stop with its length.[27] Jinkyu Kim emphasizes the significance of the placement of this psalm at the end of this collection.[28] He, along with Allen, identifies a pattern in Book V of the placement of royal psalms at the end of psalm groupings (i.e., the Songs of Ascents and the Last Davidic Psalter).[29] These royal psalms serve an important function in the interpretation of the psalm groups. In my own analysis, his observations have proved accurate regarding the placement of Pss 132 and 144 within their respective groups.

Many of the key themes within the Songs of Ascents converge and find clarity in Ps 132. In fact, the "prophetic oracle of salvation" in vv. 11–18 is probably the key passage for a proper understanding of the Songs of Ascents.[30] It is beyond the scope of this work to offer a detailed analysis of this psalm, but it is crucial to acknowledge the significance of this psalm and therefore examine how it influences an appropriate reading of Pss 135–137.

When compared to Pss 135–137, Ps 132 exhibits several significant parallels with Ps 137. With its opening imperative (זכור־יהוה לדוד ["Remember, O Yahweh, David"]), Ps 132 participates in the remembrance motif found in Pss 135–137, especially when one considers that Ps 132:1 contains the only occurrence of the root זכר ("remember") in the Songs of Ascents. In Ps 137:7, the psalmist implores Yahweh to remember the sons of Edom (i.e., in judgment). The request in Ps 132:1 is the opposite.[31] The psalmist asks Yahweh to remember David, that is, his covenant that he made with David. Could it be that Yahweh's remembrance of the Davidic

---

27. Ballhorn (ibid., 252) notes that Ps 132 is also distinct linguistically.

28. Kim, "The Strategic Arrangement."

29. Kim (ibid., 157) also points out that these psalms are followed "by a doxological psalm or a group of doxological psalms." Cf. Allen, *Psalms 101–150*, 76.

30. Crow, *Songs of Ascents*, 104.

31. Crow (ibid., 100) and Allen (*Psalms 101–150*, 308) make this connection as well.

Covenant and his remembrance of Israel's enemies refer to the same event? Such appears to be the case especially in light of Ps 132:18, which states that Yahweh will clothe the enemies of his Davidic king with shame.

The dominance of Zion in Pss 132 and 137 reinforces this parallel. Both focus extensively on Zion: Ps 132 on the Lord's choice of and future blessing of Zion when he establishes his Davidic king; Ps 137 on the grief that accompanied the exiles when they were removed from Zion and ruled by their enemies. Such a contrast indicates the need for Yahweh to install the Davidic king of Ps 132 and thus restore peace to Zion by shaming his enemies.

The prayer against Edom and Babylon, Israel's "eschatological enemies that loom larger than life,"[32] in Ps 137:7–9 echoes the affirmation at the end of Ps 132: אויביו אלביש בשת ("I will clothe his enemies with shame") (v. 18). As Yahweh had delivered Israel from their enemies in the past (Pss 135–136), so he will deliver them in the future, but Yahweh's exaltation of a Davidic king (132:17–18) will be the centerpiece of this future deliverance. Therefore, the opening prayer of Ps 132 (זכור־יהוה לדוד ["Remember, O Yahweh, David"]) and the prayer of Ps 137:7 (זכר יהוה לבני אדום ["Remember, O Yahweh, the sons of Edom"]) are prayers for the same eschatological episode in which Yahweh will exalt his Davidic king and render judgment on his enemies.

Summary of Relationship between Psalms 135–137 and the Songs of Ascents

The editorial stitching of Pss 135–137 to Pss 133–134 invites us to read Pss 135–136 in light of the Songs of Ascents. As a doxological conclusion to the Songs of Ascents,[33] Ps 134 calls for the priestly ministers to bless Yahweh. Undoubtedly, this praise was the result of the prophecy concerning Yahweh's future blessing on Zion at the time of the ultimate Davidic King (Ps 132:11–18). Psalms 135–136, with their numerous connections to Ps 134, reiterate the call to praise, but focus that call in a different direction. Instead of highlighting Yahweh's future postexilic work (as do Pss 132–134),[34] they

---

32. Allen, *Psalms 101–150*, 78. See also Goldingay, *Psalms 90–150*, 101.

33. Grossberg, *Centripetal and Centrifugal Structures*, 19.

34. In such a reading, Ps 133 does not represent family relationships, but "the reunification of the country" (the northern and southern kingdom) at Zion (see Berlin, "On the Interpretation of Psalm 133," 145). Cf. McCann, *NIB*, 4:1214 and Ḥakham, *Psalms*

recall Yahweh's past (preexilic) works as a reason for praise.[35] Psalm 135 also moves beyond the temple ministers (Ps 134) and invites all of Yahweh's servants to praise him (vv. 1-2, 20) for his superiority over all other gods (Pss 135:5; 136:2-4). Because of Yahweh's greatness, his servants should praise him from Zion (Ps 135:21), the place from which Yahweh's blessings proceed (Songs of Ascents) and where Yahweh will install his victorious Davidic king (Ps 132:13-18), thus bringing the ultimate peace to Israel/Jerusalem (Pss 122, 125, and 128).

The calls for praise in Pss 134-136 are met with a different type of call in Ps 137. The recollection of the recent exile in Babylon prompts the psalmist to reaffirm his loyalty to Jerusalem (vv. 5-6; cf. Ps 122) and to call on Yahweh to judge Israel's enemies who had attacked Jerusalem (vv. 7-9). The renewed focus on Zion (vv. 1-4) indicates that as long as Zion's enemies remained, praise could not go out from her (Ps 135:21). Thus, Ps 137 presents the problem of Israel's enemies whom Yahweh still has not shamed before the Davidic king (Ps 132:18). Instead of calling on Yahweh to remember David (Ps 132:1), the psalmist exhorts Yahweh to remember Israel's enemies (vv. 7-9).

PSALMS 135-137 IN RELATION TO THE LAST DAVIDIC PSALTER

The Last Davidic Psalter is the title of the eight Davidic psalms that follow Pss 135-137 and precede the hallelujah conclusion of the Psalter (Pss 146-150). As with the Songs of Ascents, the following examination will seek to determine how this psalm group contributes to a proper understanding of Pss 135-137. This discussion contains three major sections: 1) Connections at the Seam: Psalm 138 and Psalms 135-137, 2) An Overview of the Last Davidic Psalter, and 3) Psalm 144: Its Significance and Connections to Psalms 135-137.

101-150, 359. Also, Ps 134 represents the praise which should come from the priests who are clothed with salvation (Ps 132:16).

35. McCann (*NIB*, 4:1219) and Hossfeld and Zenger (*Psalms*, 489) identify Pss 135-136 as an explanation of Ps 134 since Ps 134 does not give reasons for praise. Hossfeld and Zenger (509) write, "they [Psalms 135-136] are a reminder of how the pilgrimages became possible: because Yhwh saved Israel out of and in the face of hostile power and give [sic] it this land with Zion/Jerusalem at its center."

PART 2: THE CONTEXT OF PSALMS 135–137

Connections at the Seam: Psalm 138 and Psalms 135–137

Unlike the seam between Pss 135–137 and the Songs of Ascents where the parallels between the groups primarily related to Ps 135, the opening psalm (Ps 138) of the last Davidic Psalter has several significant parallels with all three psalms in the psalm group 135–137. For a list of these parallels, see table 8 below. It thus appears that the editors intended this psalm to be read in light of all three psalms (135–137) and not simply Ps 137.

Table 8. Lexical Parallels between Psalms 135–137 and 138

Psalm 135–137	Psalm 138
ידה (136:1–3, 26)	ידה (vv. 1–2, 4)
אלהים (135:5); אלהי האלהים (136:2)	אלהים (v. 1)
זמר (135:3)	זמר (v. 1)
חסד (refrain of 136)	חסד (vv. 2, 8)
שם (135:1, 3)	שם (v. 2)
פה (135:16–17)	פה (v. 4)
שיר (137:3–4)	שיר (v. 5)
גדול (135:5; 136:4)	גדול (v. 5)
שפל (136:23)	שפל (v. 6)
צר (136:24)	צרה (v. 7)
אף (135:17)	אף (v. 7)
יד (136:12)	יד (v. 7)
ימין (137:5)	ימין (v. 7)
לעולם (135:13; refrain of 136); לדר־ודר (135:13)	לעולם (v. 8)
מעשׂה יד (135:15)	מעשׂה יד (v. 8)

Psalm 138 begins with the psalmist's proclamation of praise to Yahweh (vv. 1–3). Twice in the opening stanza the psalmist gives thanks to Yahweh (vv. 1–2). This twofold use of ידה ("give thanks") represents an act of obedience to the commands in the frame of Ps 136 frame (vv. 1–3, 26).[36] In addition, the reference to אלהים ("gods") in v. 1 relates back to the title אלהי האלהים ("God of gods") in Ps 136:2 and the statement of Yahweh's superior

---

36. Brennan, "Hidden Harmonies," 143; Hossfeld and Zenger, *Psalms*, 531; Ḥakham, *Psalms 101–150*, 399.

Psalms 135–137 in the Context of Book V

greatness in comparison to all gods in Ps 135:5.[37] The psalmist thus fulfills the commands of Ps 136:1–3, 26[38] in a manner that underscores Yahweh's superiority over other gods, i.e., he does it in the presence of these so-called gods. In addition, one of the reasons for his praise in Ps 138 is Yahweh's חסד ("loving-kindness") (v. 2), the central attribute in Ps 136 (i.e., the refrain).[39]

The psalmist also describes his action toward Yahweh with the verb זמר ("sing") (v. 1) and mentions Yahweh's שׁם ("name") twice in v. 2. In Ps 135 the psalmist commands the people to praise (v. 1) and sing (זמר) (v. 3) to Yahweh's שׁם ("name") (this lexeme appears twice in Ps 135:1–3).[40]

The second stanza of Ps 138 is not about the psalmist's praise of Yahweh, but the kings of the earth singing and giving thanks to Yahweh. These kings have obviously heeded the example of the kings whose defeat at the hands of Yahweh Ps 135–136 recount. The first two verses (vv. 4–5) open with a description of the future activity of the kings of the earth using language reminiscent of Pss 136–137.[41] Verse 4 opens with the third instance of the verb ידה ("give thanks") in the psalm, and v. 5 takes up the verb שׁיר ("sing"), which appears several times in Ps 137.[42] Like the psalmist, the kings of the earth will one day obey the commands of Ps 136:1–3, 21. In other words, they will be עבדי יהוה ("servants of Yahweh") (Ps 135:1). In addition, they will sing of Yahweh's ways (Ps 138:5) instead of mocking his people by asking them to sing joyful songs (Ps 137:3–4). Joseph Brennan's comments on this contrast between Psalms 137 and 138 are helpful:

> But what is most moving about this Psalm is the way in which "the kings of the earth" are portrayed as "singing of the ways of Yahweh" (v. 5), whereas in 137, 3–6 the exiled Israelites had been taunted by their captors to sing them one of Yahweh's songs. The answer to their question: "how shall we sing Yahweh's song on alien soil" (137, 4) is given in 138. When the rulers of the nations themselves sing the glories of Yahweh the God of Israel, there will no longer be any alien soil anywhere![43]

---

37. Hossfeld and Zenger, *Psalms*, 531; McCann, *NIB*, 4:1231. The use of אלהים to refer to other gods is rare in the Psalter (Pss 82:1, 6; 95:3; 96:4; 97:7), particularly in Book 5 (Pss 136:2; 138:1).

38. McCann, *NIB*, 4:1231.

39. Hossfeld and Zenger, *Psalms*, 531.

40. Ibid. McCann, *NIB*, 4:1231.

41. Hossfeld and Zenger, *Psalms*, 531.

42. Creach, *Yahweh as Refuge*, 101; Ballhorn, *Zum Telos*, 261.

43. Brennan, "Hidden Harmonies," 143. See also Wilson, *Editing*, 221–22.

Part 2: The Context of Psalms 135–137

The psalmist gives reasons for the kings' thankful singing to Yahweh in three כי ("for") clauses (vv. 4–6). Each of these motive clauses picks up on aspects of Pss 135–137. The first reason for their praise of Yahweh appears in v. 4: כי שמעו אמרי־פיך ("for they will hear the words of your mouth"). This reference to Yahweh's mouth contrasts with the description of עצבי הגוים ("idols of the nations") in Ps 135:15–18, where the idols have mouths but cannot speak (v. 16) because there is no breath in their mouth (v. 17). Not so with Yahweh; his mouth speaks and, as a result, the kings of the earth will one day turn from their idols and sing his praises (Ps 138:4–5). Such a turning will lead them to life instead of death (Ps 135:18).

The second reason for the kings' praise of Yahweh appears in v. 5: כי גדול כבוד יהוה ("for great is the glory of Yahweh"). The use of the adjective גדול ("great") repeats a similar emphasis found in Pss 135–136.[44] In both these psalms, the thematic verse of their bodies uses this adjective to establish Yahweh's superiority over other gods. Psalm 136:4 focuses on his ability to do great wonders, while in Ps 135:5, the psalmist describes his greatness in terms that are more general. Again, it appears that the kings of the earth will realize what Pss 135–136 underscore, that is, Yahweh's greatness sets him apart and thereby merits adoration.

The third reason for the kings' praise of Yahweh is found in v. 6. Particularly important for the present investigation is the first colon of this verse: כי־רם יהוה ושפל יראה ("for Yahweh is exalted and he sees the lowly"). The mention of Yahweh's concern for the lowly (שפל) recalls his remembrance of his people in their lowly estate (שבשפלנו) in Ps 136:23.[45] Just as Ps 136:24 describes this remembrance in terms of his opposition toward Israel's enemies, so Ps 138:6 contrasts his care for the lowly with his distance from the haughty (וגבה ממרחק יידע ["and he knows the haughty from afar"]). Although Ps 138 speaks in more universal terms, the connection between Israel's lowliness and the lowly in general shows, once again, the similarities between the future praise of the kings of the earth (Ps 138:4–6) and the praise expected of Israel (Ps 136).

In the final stanza of Ps 138, the psalmist once again focuses on Yahweh's work in his life. In v. 7 the psalmist mentions his distress (צרה) and his enemies (איבי).[46] The former is from the same root as צר ("adversary") in Ps

---

44. McCann, *NIB*, 4:1231.

45. Hossfeld and Zenger, *Psalms*, 531; Ḥakham, *Psalms 101–150*, 399.

46. The distress caused by enemies becomes a key theme in the Last Davidic Psalter. Babylon and Edom, who appear at the end of Ps 137, serve as pre-eminent examples of

136:24 and the latter is a synonym of this same lexeme,[47] thereby drawing together the psalmist's enemies (Ps 138) and Israel's enemies (Pss 135–137). Furthermore, the anthropomorphic description of Yahweh's deliverance of the psalmist (תשלח ידך ["you sent your hand"]) in v. 7 continues the "grasping" motif of Pss 136:24 and 137:9 (highlighted in the previous chapter). As a result, the psalmist casts his own experience of Yahweh's deliverance in language reminiscent of Yahweh's deliverance of his people (Ps 136:23–24).

The final colon of v. 7 has an important connection with Ps 137:5.[48] In his self-curse of Ps 137:5, the psalmist wishes that his right hand (ימין ["right hand"]) would cease its normal functions if he ever forgets Jerusalem. In contrast, Ps 138:7 affirms that Yahweh's right hand saves the psalmist from his enemies. The psalmist's right hand is therefore spared because Yahweh's right hand is able to save.

The last verse of Ps 138 brings to a close the parallels with Pss 135–137 with two significant connections. First, the psalmist's affirmation in the second colon, יהוה חסדך לעולם ("O Yahweh, your loving-kindness is to forever"), is almost a direct quotation of the refrain of Ps 136, the only difference being the switch from third person to second person.[49] Second, the phrase מעשי ידיך ("work of your hands") in the third colon of v. 8 continues the contrast between Yahweh and the idols, which was first highlighted in v. 4. Psalm 135:15 characterizes the nations' idols as מעשה ידי אדם ("work of human hands"). Their inability to hear, see, act, or speak relates to this characterization. They cannot do anything because they are man-made. In Ps 138:8, the works of Yahweh's hands are so important and precious to the psalmist that he petitions Yahweh never to abandon them.[50]

Overview of the Last Davidic Psalter

In contrast to most of the Songs of Ascents and Pss 135–137, the first person singular perspective dominates the Last Davidic Psalter. The majority of these psalms consist of an individual praying to Yahweh for deliverance from the distress that his enemies cause. The first indication of this theme

---

these enemies.

47. Allen, *Psalms 101–150*, 78.
48. Ḥakham, *Psalms 101–150*, 399.
49. Ibid.; Hossfeld and Zenger, *Psalmen 101–150*, 699.
50. Yahweh's works appear in the Last David Psalter often: Pss 139:14; 143:5; 145:4, 9, 10, 17.

PART 2: THE CONTEXT OF PSALMS 135-137

appears in Ps 138:7 where the psalmist affirms that Yahweh would deliver him from his distress (צרה).[51] The psalmist portrays this deliverance as exaltation over his enemies (תחיני על אף איבי ["you cause me to live over the wrath of my enemies"]).[52] The use of the particle אם ("if") puts this verse in the realm of possibility, but Pss 140–143 affirm that this possibility will indeed become a reality.

That Pss 140–143 have such a consistent theme that reaches back to Ps 138:7 raises the question of the placement of Ps 139. Psalm 139 is the longest psalm in this psalm group and deals primarily with Yahweh's extensive knowledge of the psalmist and his ways. The six-fold repetition of the root ידע ("know") (vv. 1, 2, 4, 14, 23 [x2]) underscores Yahweh's knowledge of the psalmist's ways. The use of this root establishes a contrast with Ps 138:6, where Yahweh's knowledge of the haughty is distant (וגבה ממרחק יידע ["and he knows the haughty from afar"]). Thus, the psalmist serves as an example of the lowly one mentioned in Ps 138:6 (ושפל יראה ["and he sees the lowly"]).

A second important parallel between Pss 138 and 139 revolves around the psalmist's enemies. As previously mentioned, the potential distress of the palmist in Ps 138 relates to his enemies. These enemies take center stage in Ps 139:19–22, where the psalmist emphasizes his hatred of Yahweh's enemies. He even confesses that they are his enemies simply because they are Yahweh's enemies (vv. 21–22). This becomes important in Pss 140–143. As the psalmist cries out to Yahweh from the midst of his enemies, one must remember why they are his enemies, viz., because they are Yahweh's enemies.[53]

Psalms 140–143 form a distinct thematic unit in the center of the Last Davidic Psalter.[54] Each of these psalms consists of a prayer from a distressed individual who is suffering at the hands of his enemies. In each psalm,

---

51. Brennan ("Hidden Harmonies," 143) states, "Just as the enthusiasm and gratitude of 135 and 136 were tempered by the bitter memories of the past and the fears for the future described in 137, so in 138 the dominant note of confidence and security is tinged by a gnawing realization of still-threatening danger and of anxiety for the future (vv. 6–8)."

52. The last appearance of איב was in Ps 132:18, where the psalmist affirms that Yahweh will clothe the enemies of his Davidic king with shame.

53. I identify the individual sufferer in the Last Davidic Psalter as the Davidic servant in Ps 144 (see discussion below). Such a connection between Yahweh's enemies and the enemies of the Davidic servant echoes Ps 2, where the nations are revolting against Yahweh and his anointed king.

54. Brennan, "Hidden Harmonies," 144. See also Allen, *Psalms 101–150*, 77.

Psalms 135–137 in the Context of Book V

the titles that describe these enemies demonstrate some variety, but their common activity of opposing the psalmist remains consistent. Accompanying the psalmist's prayer for deliverance in these psalms is a corresponding prayer for Yahweh's judgment of the psalmist's enemies.[55]

In addition to the psalmist and his enemies, another group within Pss 140–143 is the righteous ones. The first mention of the righteous comes at the end of Ps 140, where the psalmist confesses: אך צדיקים יודו לשמך ישבו ישרים את־פניך ("indeed, the righteous will give thanks to your name; the upright will dwell before you") (v. 14). This connects the righteous to the individual who in Ps 138:2 confessed: ואודה את־שמך ("and I will give thanks to your name"). The references to the righteous in Pss 141–142 further highlight this close relationship between the psalmist and the righteous. In Ps 141:5, the psalmist asks for a righteous man to smite and rebuke him. Such a blow would serve as an act of חסד ("loving-kindness") to the psalmist. In Ps 142:8 the psalmist connects his deliverance from his persecutors to the righteous surrounding him.[56] In contrast, Ps 143 lacks any reference to the righteous ones. In fact, this psalm affirms that there is no one who does righteousness (v. 2); instead, the psalmist pleads for deliverance based on Yahweh's righteousness (vv. 1, 11).

Psalm 144 is a pivotal psalm in the Last Davidic Psalter, and even on the higher level of Book V.[57] This psalm begins (ברוך יהוה ["blessed be Yahweh"]) in a far different tone than that of Pss 140–143,[58] recalling the last appearance of such a blessing in Ps 135:21. Yet it also includes prayers for Yahweh to deliver the psalmist from his enemies (in this case, בני נכר ["foreigners"] [vv. 7, 11]).[59] One of these prayers actually appears twice (vv. 7–8 and 11).[60] The verses that follow each occurrence of this prayer identify the

---

55. The only exception is Ps 142. It contains a prayer for deliverance but does not mention Yahweh's judgment of the psalmist's enemies. The passages that contain a prayer for Yahweh to judge the enemies of the psalmist are as follows: 140:9–12; 141:10; and 143:12.

56. In fact, the reason he is surrounded by the righteous is because he is doing the same thing they are doing, i.e., giving thanks to the name of Yahweh (cf. Pss 142:8 and 140:14).

57. Allen (*Psalms 101–150*, 76) connects Ps 144 to Pss 110 and 132 as royal psalms that are positioned at the end of their respective groups. See also Jinkyu Kim, "Strategic."

58. Brennan, "Hidden Harmonies," 7.

59. Brennan (ibid.) writes: "Nevertheless, the change in mood in this Psalm is in distinct contrast with 140–143."

60. The prayer as recorded in v. 11 is as follows: פצני והצילני מיד בני־נכר אשר פיהם דבר־שוא וימינם ימין שקר. Verses 7–8 contain some elements that are absent from v. 11.

results of Yahweh's answer to this prayer.[61] Hence, this psalm outlines two sets of events that will follow Yahweh's deliverance of the psalmist. First, the psalmist confesses in vv. 9–10 that he will sing a "new song" on musical instruments. The most significant aspect of this confession is the description of Yahweh in v. 10: הנותן תשועה למלכים הפוצה את־דוד עבדו מחרב רעה ("the one who gives salvation to kings; the one who frees David his servant from the evil sword").[62] The reference to David as עבדו ("his servant") (along with the focus on David in the superscriptions)[63] connects David to the individual of Ps 143 (and subsequently the rest of this group) who proclaims כי אני עבדך ("for I am your servant") (v. 12).[64] Furthermore, the verbal root that describes Yahweh's rescue of the Davidic servant in v. 10 (פצה ["the one who frees"]) also appears in the twice-repeated prayer of this psalm (vv. 7–8 and 11), further enhancing the identification of the individual as the Davidic servant.

The second result of Yahweh's deliverance is the blessing of the people (vv. 12–15).[65] Yahweh's blessings on the people in this psalm are in language reminiscent of Pss 127–128, psalms in which a fruitful home and the peace of Israel are examples of Yahweh's blessings (Ps 128:5).[66] Much like Ps 132 connects the peace and blessing of Israel to the establishment of the Davidic covenant, so Ps 144 links the deliverance of the suffering Davidic servant from his enemies to this same blessing upon Israel.

---

61. McCann (*NIB*, 4:1256) interprets vv. 9–10 as "the proper response" to the "new divine appearance and a new deliverance" of Ps 144.

62. Allen (*Psalms 101–150*, 364) and Goulder (*Psalms of the Return*, 275) both identify these kings as the kings of Judah who followed David. However, the positive picture of the "kings of the earth" in Ps 138 does raise the question of whether a broader group of kings could be in view here.

63. Hossfeld and Zenger (*Psalms*, 6) speak of a "Davidizing" of the Last Davidic Psalter by means of the superscriptions that attribute these psalms to David.

64. This nomenclature also echoes the reference to David as Yahweh's servant in Ps 132:10.

65. Creach (*Yahweh as Refuge*, 101) sees in Ps 144:14 ("May there be no breach, not exile") "the exilic situation."

66. The similarities include the mention of sons (Pss 127:3, 4; 128:3, 6; 144:12), plant/fruit imagery (פרי הבטן in Ps 127:3; בניך כשתלי זיתים and אשתך כגפן פריה in Ps 128:3; בנינו כנטעים מגדלים in Ps 144:12; and מזוינו מלאים in Ps 144:13), and the peace of Jerusalem/Israel (וראה בטוב ירושלם כל ימי חייך in Ps 128:5; שלום על־ישראל in Ps 128:6; and אין־פרץ ואין יוצאת ואין צוחה ברחבתינו in Ps 144:14).

Psalms 135–137 in the Context of Book V

Psalm 145 completes the Last Davidic Psalter with a confession of praise that draws together many of the themes of Book V.[67] This psalm "serves to prepare the way for the substance of praise in Pss 146–50,"[68] affirming King Yahweh's gracious care and provision for those who hope in him and his destruction of the wicked. For this reason, "all flesh will bless his holy name for forever and ever" (Ps 145:21).[69]

Psalm 144: Its Significance and Connections to Psalms 135–137

In a manner almost identical to that of Ps 132, Ps 144 serves a crucial role in properly understanding the Last Davidic Psalter, and because of its location, the entirety of Book V. As was evident in the above overview, much of its theological weight directly relates to the mention of the suffering Davidic servant. In connecting the people's ultimate blessing to the deliverance of this Davidic servant from his enemies, the psalm demonstrates that Israel's hope is not tied simply to their deliverance from their enemies, but to this servant's deliverance from his enemies. In what follows, I outline the relationship between Ps 144 and Pss 135–137.

There are several important parallels between Pss 144 and 137. First, the psalmist requests rescue from בני נכר ("foreigners") (vv. 7, 11). The only other occurrence of the adjective נכר ("foreign") in Book V is located in Ps 137:4, where the people recall their own suffering in a foreign land (אדמת נכר ["foreign soil"]). Furthermore, the psalmist's confession of praise in v. 9 (אלהים שיר חדש אשירה לך בנבל עשׂור אזמרה־לך ["O God, I will sing a new song to you; on a ten-stringed harp I will sing to you"]) echoes Ps 137:4, where the captives wonder how they could sing a שיר־יהוה ("song of

---

67. Wilson (*Editing*, 225) designates this psalm the "climax" of Book V. Wilson uses the emphasis in Ps 145 on Yahweh as King to support his theory that Books IV and V urge readers of the Psalter to trust in Yahweh alone as King in contrast to an earthly Davidic king (pp. 225–27; see also idem, "Shaping the Psalter," 80–81). Unfortunately, Wilson and those who follow his lead in this matter (e.g., McCann, "Books I–III" and idem, *NIB*, 4:1258–59) have constructed a contrast out of what should be a confluence of these two themes. The emphasis on Yahweh's kingship is for creating hope in his future establishment of the Davidic king as his earthly vice-regent. Such is apparent when one considers the strategic placement of royal psalms in Book V as outlined in this chapter. For a thorough critique of Wilson's understanding of Book V, see Snearly, "Return." Cf. Grant, *King*, 33–39.

68. Allen, *Psalms 101–150*, 77.

69. The phrase כל־בשׂר only occurs twice in Book V (here and in Ps 136:25).

Part 2: The Context of Psalms 135–137

Yahweh") in a foreign land.[70] In contrast, the psalmist now sings שיר חדש ("a new song") and even pulls out his musical instrument (v. 9). Musical instruments were hung in the trees in Babylon (Ps 137:2), but in Ps 144:9 the psalmist uses them to accompany his new song.

Another significant parallel between Pss 137 and 144 is the concluding double blessing (אשרי in 137:8–9 and 144:15) in each psalm.[71] Psalm 144:15 pronounces a blessing on the people whose God is Yahweh and to whom the events of vv. 12–14 apply.[72] In Ps 137:8–9 the one who recompenses the enemies of Jerusalem is blessed. Read in the context of Book V (i.e., Pss 132 and 144), this connection further underscores the connection between the peace of Israel and Yahweh's judgment of the enemies of his Davidic king.

These parallels between Pss 137 and 144 raise important questions regarding the implications of these connections. As Leopold Sabourin rightly notes, the main theme of Pss 137–144 is "prayers for help against enemies, among whom Edom and Babylon occupied the first rank."[73] Even so, there is a major difference between Ps 137, which focuses on the enemies of Israel, and Pss 138–144, which are concerned with the enemies of the individual speaker. So, the question becomes: How do these two sets of enemies relate?

The answer given by most commentators is that the individual "'David,' in the headings of the ... psalms" simply serves "as representative of the community"[74] (democratization). In other words, the people were

---

70. Zenger, "Composition and Theology," 96.

71. This accounts for four of the eleven appearances of אשרי in Book V of the Psalter. The other appearances are 112:1; 119:1, 2; 127:5; 128:1, 2; 146:5.

72. Ballhorn, *Zum Telos*, 261.

73. Sabourin, *The Psalms*, 184. See also Allen, *Psalms 101–150*, 77–8.

74. Allen, *Psalms 101–150*, 78. Cf. Brennan, "Hidden Harmonies," 144ff.; Wilson, *Editing*, 221; Creach, *Yahweh as Refuge*, 101; James Luther Mays, *Psalms*, 436–437; McCann, *NIB*, 4:1255. What drives Mays and McCann to such an explanation is the numerous repetitions of Ps 18 in this psalm. One may question why a psalm over one hundred psalms removed carries more weight than the immediate context. The influence of Wilson's proposal regarding the failure of the Davidic Covenant is also a factor in such an interpretation (See McCann, *NIB*, 4:1255). Such an interpretation hardly does justice to the importance of Pss 110, 132, and 144 in Book V of the Psalter. As has been demonstrated, Pss 132 and 144 focus the theology of their respective groups on the Davidic king.

The present interpretation agrees with Ḥakham (*Psalms 101–150*, 445), who states, "From here [v. 12] until the end of the psalm, the psalmist describes the peace that will reign after his rescue from the hands of his enemies." Although Ḥakham does not read this psalm eschatologically, he does interpret the blessings of the people as the result of "using David's prayers as their prayers."[75] While such an interpretation is possible, it does not go far enough in explaining the centrality of the Davidic figure in Ps 144 (and in the superscriptions).[76] Why does the psalm explicitly identify the one praying as the Davidic servant? The linking of the individual to the Davidic servant (vv. 10–11) is very suspect considering the pattern already witnessed in the Songs of Ascents, where Ps 132 was placed at the end of the group for the purpose of making the Davidic king central to the message of the group and thus the eschatological restoration of Israel.

Furthermore, this type of explanation does not take seriously the drastic change from a collective perspective (evident in the majority of psalms in the Songs of Ascents and Pss 135–137) to the individual perspective (Pss 138–145). If the editor(s) wanted to focus solely on the community, why emphasize an individual sufferer at the end of the Psalter? Instead, Pss 138–145 urge readers to question why this individual sufferer comes to the forefront at the end of a book (Book V) dominated by corporate psalms.

The solution to this problem relates to the importance of reading Pss 137 and 144 properly. Allen correctly identifies one of the purposes of Ps 137 as the provision of "a hermeneutical interpretation for these enemies identifying them as a veritable Babylon and Edom, eschatological enemies that loom larger than life."[77] Certainly, the location of Ps 137 leads readers to interpret the enemies of Pss 138–145 as more than just individuals, but as nations such as Babylon and Edom. But the most important question is: Whose enemies are they?

The answer of Ps 144 is that they are enemies of the Davidic servant, not just Israel. Hence, as Israel begged for judgment on their enemies (Ps 137), they are reminded that their enemies would become the enemies of the Davidic servant (Pss 138–145). The enemies of this suffering Davidic servant would not simply be individuals who oppose him, but they would be nations like Babylon and Edom who would oppose not only him but also Yahweh (Ps 139:19–22).[78] Thus, before Israel could experience ultimate vic-

---

the king's deliverance. Kim ("Strategic," 157) goes one step further and reads the psalm eschatologically: "In my opinion, vv. 12–15 portray a scene of eschatological blessings under the messianic king."

75. Mays, *Psalms*, 437.

76. Grant (*King*, 33–39, 280–89) demonstrates that these two interpretations (eschatological and democratization) are not mutually exclusively.

77. Allen, *Psalms 101–150*, 78. Cf. Goldingay, *Psalms 90–150*, 601.

78. This reading corresponds to Ps 2, where the nations of the earth are revolting

tory over their enemies, the individual Davidic servant must himself suffer at the hands of his enemies. His deliverance results in the deliverance of the people of Israel, blessings on their households, and the peace of Israel/Jerusalem. Therefore, Ps 144 brings resolution to many of the problems presented in Book V of the Psalter. Fittingly, the praise of Yahweh in Ps 145 and then the doxology for the entire Psalter (Pss 146–150) follow this pivotal psalm. The answer for all of Israel's distress and the key for their ultimate blessing revolve around Yahweh's deliverance of the suffering Davidic servant from his enemies. And since Book V reflects the postexilic situation of Israel, this Davidic servant is not a current ruler, but is the future Davidic king whose successful reign is reflected in Pss 110 and 132. Because Yahweh is king (Ps 145:1), Israel can be confident that he will ultimately restore his people through his promised Davidic servant-king.

PSALMS 135–137 AND THE STRUCTURE OF BOOK V

Now that I have outlined the theological function of Pss 135–137 in their canonical context, it is appropriate to take one final step and investigate how these three psalms fit into the structure of Book V. One of the primary focal points in canonical studies of the Psalter is the identification of the structure of each of its five books. The limitations of the present study prevent a proposal for the overall structure of Book V.[79] However, one may deduce observations regarding Pss 135–137 and their role in the overall structure of Book V from the above contextual analysis of these three psalms.

When deciphering the structure of a large portion of texts, the key issue is one's criteria for division. In some respects, one can develop these criteria only as one works through the contents of the text. In Psalter studies, scholars have used several criteria in delineating the structure of the books of the Psalter. These criteria include superscriptions, psalm types/forms, lexical parallels, thematic parallels, structural parallels, or a combination of one or more of the aforementioned items.

There have been several different proposals regarding the role of Pss 135–137 in the structure of Book V. In his original proposal, Wilson's primary criterion was the placement of hallelujah psalms at the end of major

---

against Yahweh and his Davidic king.

79. Such a proposal is only possible after a thorough analysis of the entire book. For a good overview of various proposals for Book V, see Snearly, "Return," 8–47.

sections and hodu psalms at the beginning of sections.[80] Thus, Wilson separated Ps 135 from Ps 136, identifying the former as a conclusion to the Songs of Ascents and the latter as an introduction to the psalm group 136–150.[81] Others, such as Allen and Leuenberger, have followed Wilson's original proposal.[82]

A more popular option has been to place a division between Pss 136 and 137. Typically, proponents of this division recognize (as I have demonstrated) that Ps 136 is the twin of Ps 135, and we therefore should not separate these two psalms. Many who espouse this division identify Pss 135–136 as an addendum or appendix to the Songs of Ascents.[83] Some regard Ps 137 as a stand-alone psalm functioning as a bridge to the Last Davidic Psalter.[84] Others see Ps 137 as introducing the Last Davidic Psalter.[85]

On rare occasions, scholars have kept all three psalms (Pss 135–137) together and attached them to either the Songs of Ascents[86] or the Last Davidic Psalter.[87] In this regard, I propose reading Pss 135–137 as a unit, but I do not incorporate this unit into either of its surrounding groups.[88] Therefore, Pss 135–137, as a whole, bridges the two larger groups that surround it.

There are several reasons for this proposal. First, one of the primary justifications for the attachment of Pss 135–136 to the Songs of Ascents is the amount of lexical repetition between Pss 134 and 135. What many fail to realize is that the brevity of Ps 134 makes the repetition appear overwhelmingly significant. With only 23 words (excluding the superscription), it would have been very easy to repeat 14 of these words in a psalm the length of Ps 135 (21 verses).[89] In fact, there are more parallels between Pss

---

80. Wilson, *Editing*, 186–90.

81. Ibid., 188–90.

82. Allen, *Psalms 101–150*, 75; Leuenberger, *Konzeptionen*, 320.

83. Cho, "Hallelujah Psalms," 118; Ballhorn, *Zum Telos*, 262; Hossfeld and Zenger, *Psalms*, 5.

84. Ballhorn, *Zum Telos*, 260–61; Hossfeld and Zenger, *Psalms*, 520.

85. Brennan, "Hidden Harmonies," 128; Miller, "The End of the Psalter," 105.

86. Zenger, "Composition and Theology," 98; Snearly, "Return," 165ff.

87. Goulder, *Psalms of the Return*, 15–16; Kim, "Strategic," 150–152.

88. DeClaissé-Walford (*Reading from the Beginning*, 122–24) appears to take a similar view since she treats Pss 135–137 as a separate group.

89. In addition to its brevity, one must also take into account the twofold repetition of the command ברכו את־יהוה (vv. 1–2).

Part 2: The Context of Psalms 135–137

138 and 135–137 than there are between Psalms 134 and 135–137,[90] but because Ps 138 is longer, these parallels make up a smaller percentage of the words in that psalm. If one's primary criterion for joining or dividing adjacent psalms is lexical repetition, then one could just as easily argue for the inclusion of Pss 135–137 in the Last Davidic Psalter.[91] It appears that the editors focused on linking this psalm group with both of its bordering psalm groups. Their primary tool in doing so was lexical repetition. This lexical repetition, however, does not take priority over the use of common superscriptions in this latter portion of Book V.

90. See above. There are 18 parallels, not including the divine name יהוה. As highlighted above, Ps 138 not only parallels Ps 137 but also has many parallels with Pss 135–136.

91. In a recent attempt to argue that Pss 120–137 should be regarded as a single group, Snearly (*Return*, 143–54) critiques my proposed structure by arguing that "the links between Psalms 135–137 and the psalms that follow are strongest at the seam (with Psalm 138); the links do not continue after Psalm 138. While there may be parallels between Psalms 135–137 and 138, there are not parallels between Psalms 135–137 and 138–145 like there are parallels between Psalms 135–137 and 120–134" (150). A couple of comments are necessary in response to Snearly's analysis. First, a closer look at the data reveals numerous, significant parallels between Pss 135–137 and the Last Davidic Psalter. A brief examination of Christoph Buysch's chart of key words in Ps 138 and their repetition in the Last Davidic Psalter is helpful (see Buysch, *Der letzte Davidpsalter*, 63–64). Buysch's chart contains 27 words that appear in three or more psalms in the Last Davidic Psalter (he includes words that occur with less frequency, but I have chosen not to use them as evidence). Of these 27 words, 16 appear in Pss 135–137 (59 percent). Furthermore, an additional four of these key words have significant links with Pss 135–137 on the basis of synonymy (שמע in Pss 138:4; 141:6; 143:1, 8; 145:19 and אזן in Ps 135:17), the same root (צרה in Pss 138:7; 142:3; 143:11 and צר in Ps 136:24), or theme (איב in Pss 138:7; 139:22; 143:3, 9, 12 and ישע in Pss 138:7; 140:8; 144:10; 145:19; both touch on significant themes in Pss 135–137), thus bringings the percentage up to 74 percent. All of these parallels might not fit Snearly's arbitrary definition of a key-word link (see 1), but they definitely support more significant parallels between Pss 135–137 and the Last Davidic Psalter than Snearly suggests. Second, based on his own analysis of Pss 138–145, Snearly identifies "a prevailing motif of the group" as "the theme of kingship" (4; see also 68) (It bears mentioning that this is not one of his "key-word links" for this psalm group). Interestingly, he notes, "the vast majority of occurrences of the מלך root and its synonyms are in Psalms 135–136" (162, n. 15). In the end, Snearly's own analysis shows that Pss 135–137 relate significantly to his primary motif of *both* the Songs of Ascents (Zion) *and* the Last Davidic Psalter (kingship). Snearly's findings demonstrate three things: 1) they support reading Pss 135–137 as a bridge group between these two larger groups; 2) they show that the quality of links (i.e., kingship in Pss 135–137 and 138–145) is just as important as the quantity of links (although the quantity also applies to the connections between Pss 135–137 and both these groups); and 3) they underscore Grant's (*King*, 225–26) and Snearly's own (188) warning of the subjectivity of only using keyword linking to delineate psalm groups.

Psalms 135–137 in the Context of Book V

A second reason for the proposal to treat Pss 135–137 as a separate group is the unity of the surrounding groups. My above survey of the Songs of Ascents and the Last Davidic Psalter demonstrates three things: 1) each group has a distinct theme(s), 2) the theme(s) of each group is brought together/resolved by a psalm toward the end of the collection that highlights the Davidic king/servant, and 3) as Kim has noted,[92] each group ends with a doxological psalm (or pair of psalms). This common pattern in both groups indicates a unity that we significantly alter when we attach one or all three psalms from Pss 135–137 to one of these larger groups.[93]

Furthermore, the common superscriptions of the psalms within these groups reinforce the unity of each of these border groups. Thus, what unites Pss 135–137 the most is their lack of a superscription in the midst of two major groups united by common superscriptions. Just as Grant has underscored the disjunctive function of the absence of superscriptions in Books I–III of the Psalter,[94] so also the trend continues in the second half of Book V.

A final reason for treating Pss 135–137 as an individual group is the numerous connections between these psalms. There is no question regarding the similarities between Pss 135 and 136, thus explaining why so many structural proposals for Book V keep these two psalms together. However, my analysis has effectively demonstrated how the majority of Ps 137 relates to the two compositionally significant verses in Ps 136 (vv. 23–24). This appears to be the work of an editor(s) who positioned Ps 137 as a reaction against the positive affirmations of Pss 135–136, particularly Ps 136:23–24. Although Ps 138 is a response to Ps 137, it has an equal number of parallels with Pss 135 and 136. Therefore, Ps 138 is a reaction to all three psalms in this group, thus freeing Ps 137 to be read with Pss 135–136.

Jamie Grant makes a similar argument in his study of the structure of Book V:

> Zenger is correct in pointing out that the repetition of content from Ps 134:1–2 in Ps 135:2 does indicate linking, however, *this should not result in the inclusion of these psalms along with the Psalms of Ascents in terms of structure*. On the contrary, the superscriptions

---

92. Kim, "Strategic," 157.

93. For example, if one attaches Pss 135–136 to the Songs of Ascents, the role of Ps 132 is diminished since Pss 135–136 present new themes to the collection and also overshadow the collection by their length (the length of Ps 132 is one of the factors that distinguishes it as an editorially significant psalm within the Songs of Ascents).

94. Grant, *King*, 227–29.

Part 2: The Context of Psalms 135–137

> which head each of Psalms 120–134 fulfil both conjunctive and disjunctive functions—*the extent of the psalm grouping in question is made clear not, primarily, by the content of the psalms, but by their superscriptions.* The inclusion of elements from Ps 134 at the beginning of Ps 135 appears, once again, to be an attempt to link and legitimate, the addition of other psalmic material to a previously existing version of the Book of Psalms. (emphasis mine)[95]

With Grant, I am arguing that the primary means by which the editors of the Psalter group psalms in the latter half of Book V (after Ps 119) was the use (or non-use) of superscriptions. Such an agenda distinguishes Pss 135–137 as an individual unit with many lexical connections to the two psalm groups around it. The purpose of these lexical connections is to anchor this group as a bridge between these two larger groups. Therefore, when evaluating the structure of the second half of Book V, the lexical parallels are secondary to the psalm headings.

---

95. Ibid., 242–43.

Conclusion

IMPLICATIONS FOR PSALTER RESEARCH

Contextual study of the Psalter is an ever-evolving approach. Scholars have made great strides in methodological rigor and clarity, and no doubt will make further strides. In what follows, I outline some methodological implications gleaned from my own analysis of Pss 135–137 in hopes that these implications will inform future contextual investigations of other portions of the Psalter.

Poetic Analysis as a Prerequisite to Contextual Analysis

The present work has demonstrated the benefit of prefacing a contextual analysis of a psalm or psalm group with a detailed poetic analysis of that same psalm or psalm group. The poetic analysis of Pss 135–136 highlighted the significance of Pss 135:13–14 and 136:23–24 in the interpretation of these psalms. Notably, the primary lexical and thematic linkages between Pss 137 and 135–136 revolve around these verses. In particular, the majority of parallels between Pss 137 and 136 relate to Ps 136:23–24.

The fact that these verses were distinct on the level of the individual psalm and on the contextual level indicates something regarding the work of the editor(s) of the Psalter. It is impossible to know whether or not the editors inserted these compositionally significant verses in order to link these psalms together or whether the significance of the verses influenced their selection and placement of Ps 137. The important conclusion for interpreters of the Psalter is that compositionally significant verses can play an important role in binding psalms together and advancing the conversations between adjacent psalms.

PART 2: THE CONTEXT OF PSALMS 135–137

Importance of Interpreting Psalm Groups as Units

The position of Pss 135–137 between two different groups of psalms meant that in the present work I had to interpret not only the psalms immediately adjacent to Pss 135–137, but also the entire psalm group. Both psalm groups were united by their common superscriptions. Although the themes within both of these groups were different, their function was similar. Both the Songs of Ascents and the Last Davidic Psalter found their ultimate meaning in a psalm focused on the Davidic king (Pss 132 and 144). In each case, this psalm was located near the end of the psalm group and brought resolution to many of the groups' major themes. If I had not analyzed the psalm group as a whole, I might have missed the significance of these two psalms within their respective psalm groups and their connections with Pss 135–137.

The implication for Psalter studies is that one should first seek to treat groups of psalms with common superscriptions as a unit before interpreting them in the context of the larger Psalter.[1] Other groups within the Psalter may prove different, but in my analysis, a proper interpretation of the groups as a whole was crucial in properly adducing the function of Pss 135–137 in their canonical context. Furthermore, in the latter half of Book V, the superscriptions (or lack thereof) play an important role and serve as the primary criterion for outlining the structure of this portion of Book V.

Importance of the Seams

The editor(s) primarily bound Pss 135–137 to their border groups through numerous lexical and thematic parallels at the seams of these groups. Psalm 135 repeats most of the phrases in Ps 134 and many of the lexemes in Psalm 133. These connections bind Ps 135 to the Songs of Ascents and impose a context in which to read Pss 135–137. One can say the same about Ps 138. Psalm 138 is much longer than Ps 134 and therefore displays a smaller percentage of parallels with Pss 135–137. However, it contains many lexical and thematic parallels not only with Ps 137 but also with Pss 135–136, thus

---

1. This does not mean that one should rearrange the psalms according to common superscriptions. For example, one should not remove the psalms of the Sons of Korah (Pss 42, 44–49, 84–85, and 87–88) from their respective contexts and read them together. However, if a group of psalms is left intact by the editor(s) of the Psalter (e.g., the Songs of Ascents), one should seek to interpret this group as a unit before comparing the individual psalms to psalms outside the group.

CONCLUSION

showing that the editor(s) intended for it to be read as a response to all three psalms.

Such parallels at the borders of psalm groups indicate a high level of editorial activity. One would expect such activity if the editor(s) of the Psalter were using completed compositions in their compilation of the Psalter. Therefore, those who participate in contextual investigations of the Psalter should pay close attention to the seams between adjacent psalm groups. In his analysis of the editorial activity within the Songs of Ascents, Crow makes a similar observation: "[i]t is a truism that major additions are more likely to occur at the beginning or the end of a pericope than in the middle of one."[2] Crow's evaluation of pericopes extends to the larger level of psalm groups. The beginning and end of a psalm group are fertile grounds for editorial activity in the Psalter. Many interpretive diamonds are waiting to be mined from these seams and can only be found when one pays close attention to the lexical and thematic parallels at these joints.

CONCLUDING THOUGHTS

When I began my investigation of the contextual function of Pss 135–137, I did not expect to mention the Davidic king in my work. Yet, when I began to assess the key connections between these psalms and their bordering psalm groups, I quickly realized that the ultimate hope at the end of the Psalter rests upon Yahweh's future establishment of the Davidic Covenant, as I have demonstrated throughout this work. It is not that this emphasis surprised me; my surprise came as I realized the extent to which these psalms, which do not even mention the Davidic king, continue the conversation in the Psalter about the Davidic king. As I noted above and as others have rightly underscored, this surely deals a deadly blow to Wilson's and McCann's false dichotomy between the kingship of Yahweh and the earthly Davidic king. The people of Israel were reminded of Yahweh's kingship in order to engender trust and hope that one day Yahweh would restore their fortunes by means of his eschatological fulfillment of the Davidic Covenant.

---

2. Crow, *Songs of Ascents*, 143. Davis ("Contextual Analysis," 308–309) finds a similar pattern with adjacent psalms in Pss 107–118: "Within the Psalms 107–118 corpus, there typically are strong linkages—sometimes lexical, sometimes thematic—between the end of one psalm and the beginning of the next. These linkages function not only to bind one psalm to the next, but also to interconnect groups of psalms within the corpus that at one time may have been joined together as small independent clusters of psalms."

Part 2: The Context of Psalms 135–137

Yet this messianic emphasis has much broader implications for present readers. Just as Israel was reminded of the future extablishment of the messianic kingdom in the midst of a world revolting against Yahweh's rule, so also today the people of Jesus the Messiah still wait in anticipation for his return, his defeat of his enemies, and the consummation of his kingdom. In a world that often feels like the bad guys win (Ps 137), the Psalter continues to remind us of Yahweh's superiority over all other kings and so called "gods" (Pss 135–136) and inspires us to petition him as Israel did in their exile: "Remember, O Yahweh" (Pss 132:1; 137:7).

Bibliography

Ahn, John. "Psalm 137: Complex Communal Laments." *JBL* 127 (2008) 267–89.
Alden, Robert L. "Chiastic Psalms (III): A Study in the Mechanics of Semitic Poetry in Psalms 101–150." *JETS* 21 (1978) 199–210.
Alexander, Joseph. *The Psalms Translated and Explained*. Edinburgh: Andrew Elliot and James Thin, 1864.
Allen, Leslie C. *Psalms 101–150*. WBC 21. Revised Edition. Nashville: Thomas Nelson, 2002.
Alter, Robert. *The Art of Biblical Poetry*. New York: Basic, 1985.
———. *The Book of Psalms: A Translation with Commentary*. New York: Norton, 2007.
———. "Introduction to the Old Testament." Pages 11–35 in *The Literary Guide to the Bible*. Edited by Robert Alter and Frank Kermode. Cambridge, MA: Belknap, 1987.
Anderson, A. A. *Psalms 73–150*. NCB. London: Oliphants, 1972.
Auffret, Pierre. "Note sur la structure littéraire du Psaume CXXXVI." *VT* 27 (1977) 1–12.
———. "Ton nom pour toujours: Nouvelle étude structurelle du Psaume 135." *ScEs* 57 (2005) 229–241.
Augustine. *Expositions on the Book of Psalms: Translated with Notes and Indices*. Vol. 8 of *A Select Library of the Nicene and Post-Nicene Fathers of the Christian Church*. Edited by Philip Schaff. New York: Christian Literature, 1886.
Ballhorn, Egbert. *Zum Telos des Psalters. Der Textzusammenhang des Vierten und Fünften Psalmenbuchs (Ps 90–150)*. BBB 138. Berlin: Philo Verlagsges, 2004.
Bar Efrat, Shimon. "Love of Zion: A Literary Interpretation of Psalm 137." Pages 3–11 in *Tehillah le-Moshe: Biblical and Judaic Studies in Honor of Moshe Greenberg*. Edited by Mordechai Cogan, Barry L. Eichler, and Jeffrey H. Tigay. Winona Lake, IN: Eisenbrauns, 1997.
Barbiero, Gianni. *Das erste Psalmenbuch als Einheit: Eine synchrone Analyse von Psalm 1–41*. ÖBS 16. Frankfurt am Main: Peter Lang, 1999.
Barnes, Albert. *Notes, Critical, Explanatory, and Practical, on the Book of Psalms*. Vol. 3. New York: Harper and Brothers, 1869.
Barré, Lloyd M. "Halelû yāh: A Broken Inclusion." *CBQ* 45 (1983) 195–200.
Berlin, Adele. *The Dynamics of Biblical Parallelism*. Revised and Expanded Edition. Dearborn, MI: Dove, 2008.
———. "Psalms and the Literature of Exile: Psalms 137, 44, 69, and 78." Pages 65–86 in *The Book of Psalms: Composition and Reception*. Edited by Peter W. Flint and Patrick D. Miller. VTSup 99. Leiden: Brill, 2005.

Bibliography

Brennan, Joseph P. "Some Hidden Harmonies in the Fifth Book of Psalms." Pages 126–58 in *Essays in Honor of Joseph P. Brennan*. Edited by Robert F. McNamara. Rochester, NY: Saint Bernard's Seminary, 1976.

Briggs, Charles Augustus and Emilie Grace. *A Critical and Exegetical Commentary on the Book of Psalms*. 2 Vols. ICC. Edinburgh: T & T Clark, 1907.

Brown, W. P. *Seeing the Psalms: A Theology of Metaphor*. Louisville: Westminster John Knox, 2002.

Buysch, Christoph. *Der letzte Davidpsalter: Interpretation, Komposition und Funktion der Psalmengruppe Ps 138–145*. SBB 63. Stuttgart: Katholisches Bibelwerk, 2009.

Childs, Brevard S. *Introduction to the Old Testament as Scripture*. Philadelphia: Fortress Press, 1979.

Cho, Yong Kyu. "The Hallelujah Psalms in the Context of the Hebrew Psalter." PhD diss., The Southern Baptist Theological Seminary, 1998.

Cohen, Abraham. *The Psalms: Hebrew Text & English Translation with an Introduction and Commentary*. Revised by E. Oratz. Assisted by Shalom Shahar. London / New York: Soncino, 1992.

Cole, Robert L. "Rhetorics and Canonical Structure in the Hebrew Psalter Book III (Psalms 73–89)." PhD diss., University of California Los Angeles, 1996.

———. *The Shape and Message of Book III (Psalms 73–89)*. JSOTSup 307. Sheffield: Sheffield Academic, 2000.

Creach, Jerome F. D. *Yahweh as Refuge and the Editing of the Hebrew Psalter*. JSOTSup 217. Sheffield: Sheffield Academic, 1996.

Crow, Loren D. *The Songs of Ascents (Psalms 120 –134): Their Place in Israelite History and Religion*. SBLDS 148. Atlanta: Scholars, 1996.

Davis, Barry. "A Contextual Analysis of Psalms 107–118." PhD diss., Trinity Evangelical Divinity School, 1996.

Day, John N. "The Imprecatory Psalms and Christian Ethics." *BSac* 159 (2002) 166–86.

DeClaissé-Walford, N. L. *Reading from the Beginning: The Shaping of the Hebrew Psalter*. Macon, GA: Mercer University Press, 1997.

Delitzsch, Franz. *Biblical Commentary on the Psalms*. Vol. 3. Translated by Francis Bolton. Edinburgh: T & T Clark, 1871.

Eaton, J. H. *Psalms: Introduction and Commentary*. TBC. London: SCM Press, 1976.

Fokkelman, J. P. *Major Poems of the Hebrew Bible: At the Interface of Hermeneutics and Structural Analysis*. 4 vols. Assen: Van Gorcum, 1998.

Gerstenberger, Erhard. S. *Psalms, Part II, and Lamentations*. FOTL 15. Grand Rapids: Eerdmans, 2001.

Goldingay, John. *Psalms 90–150*. Vol. 3 of *Psalms*. Baker Commentary on the Old Testament. Grand Rapids: Baker Academic, 2008.

Goulder, Michael D. *The Psalms of the Return (Book V: Psalms 107–150): Studies in the Psalter, IV*. JSOTSup 258. Sheffield: Sheffield Academic, 1998.

Grant, Jamie A. *The King as Exemplar: The Function of Deuteronomy's Kingship Law in the Shaping of the Book of Psalms*. Academia Biblica 17. Atlanta: Society of Biblical Literature, 2004.

Grossberg, Daniel. *Centripetal and Centrifugal Structures in Biblical Poetry*. SBLMS 39. Atlanta: Scholars, 1989.

Gunkel, Hermann. *An Introduction to the Psalms*. Completed by Joachim Begrich. Translated by James D. Nogalski. Macon, GA: Mercer University Press, 1998.

Bibliography

———. *The Psalms: A Form-Critical Introduction*. Translated by Thomas M. Horner. Philadelphia: Fortress, 1967.
Ḥakham, Amos. *Psalms 101–150*. Vol. 3 of *The Bible Psalms with the Jerusalem Commentary*. The Koschitzky Edition. Jerusalem: Mosad Harav Kook, 2003.
Halle, Morris, and John J. McCarthy. "The Metrical Structure of Psalm 137." *JBL* 100 (1981) 161–67.
Hays, Christopher B. "How Shall We Sing? Psalm 137 in Historical and Canonical Context." *HBT* 27 (2005) 35–55.
Hengstenberg, Ernst Wilhelm. *Commentary on the Psalms*. Vol. 3. Translated by John Thomson Leith and Patrick Fairbairn Salton. Edinburgh: T & T Clark, 1848.
Hossfeld, Frank-Lothar and Erich Zenger. *Psalms 3: A Commentary on Psalms 101–150*. Translated by Linda M. Maloney. Hermeneia. Minneapolis: Fortress, 2011.
Howard, David M., Jr. "A Contextual Reading of Psalms 90–94." Pages 108–23 in *The Shape and Shaping of the Psalter*. Edited by J. Clinton McCann. JSOTSup 159. Sheffield: JSOT Press, 1993.
———. "The Psalms and Current Study." Pages 23–40 in *Interpreting the Psalms: Issues and Approaches*. Edited by David Firth and Philip S. Johnston. Downers Grove, IL: InterVarsity, 2005.
———. *The Structure of Psalms 93–100*. Winona Lake, IN: Eisenbrauns, 1997.
Human, Dirk J. "Psalm 136: A Liturgy with Reference to Creation and History." Pages 73–88 in *Psalms and Liturgy*. Edited by Dirk J. Human and Cas J. A. Vos. LHBOTS 410. London: T & T Clark, 2004.
Jauss, Hannelore. "Fluchpsalmen beten?: Zum Problem der Feind- und Fluchpsalmen." *BK* 51 (1996) 107–115.
Keet, Cuthbert C. *A Study of the Psalms of Ascents: A Critical and Exegetical Commentary upon Psalms CXX to CXXXIV*. London: Mitre, 1969.
Kim, Jinkyu. "The Strategic Arrangement of Royal Psalms in Books IV–V." *WTJ* 70 (2008) 143–157.
Kimḥi, David. *The Commentary of Rabbi David Kimhi on Psalms CXX–CL*. Edited and Translated by Joshua Baker and Ernest W. Nicholson. Cambridge: Cambridge University Press, 1973.
Kirkpatrick, Alexander F. *The Book of Psalms*. Cambridge: Cambridge University Press, 1906.
Kraus, Hans-Joachim. *Psalms 60–150: A Commentary*. Translated by Hilton C. Oswald. Minneapolis: Augsburg, 1989.
Kugel, James. *The Idea of Biblical Poetry: Parallelism and Its History*. New Haven, CT: Yale University, 1981.
Kuntz, J. Kenneth. "Grounds for Praise: The Nature and Function of the Motive Clause in the Hymns of the Hebrew Psalter." Pages 148–83 in *Worship and the Hebrew Bible: Essays in Honour of John T Willis*. Edited by Patrick M. Graham, Rick R. Marrs, and Steven L. McKenzie. JSOTSup 284. Sheffield: Sheffield Academic, 1999.
Laney, J. Carl. "A Fresh Look at the Imprecatory Psalms." *BSac* 138 (1981) 35–45.
Leuenberger, Martin. *Konzeptionen des Königtums Gottes im Psalter: Untersuchungen zu Komposition und Redaktion der theokratischen Bücher IV–V im Psalter*. ATANT 83. Zürich: Theologischer Verlag, 2004.
Lowth, Robert. *Lectures on the Sacred Poetry of the Hebrews*. Translated by G. Gregory. A New Edition with Notes by Calvin E. Stowe. Andover: Flagg and Gould, 1829.
Luc, Alex. "Interpreting the Curses in the Psalms." *JETS* 42 (1999) 395–410.

Bibliography

Lugt, Pieter van der. *Cantos and Strophes in Biblical Hebrew Poetry: With Special Reference to the First Book of the Psalter.* OTS 53. Leiden: Brill, 2006.

Macholz, Christian. "Psalm 136: Exegetische Beobachtungen mit methodologischen Seitenblicken." Pages 177–86 in *Mincha.* Edited by Erhard Blum. Neukirchen-Vluyn: Neukirchener Verlag, 2000.

Martin, Chalmers. "The Imprecations in the Psalms." *Princeton Theological Review* 1 (1903) 537–53.

Mathys, Hans-Peter. *Dichter und Beter: Theologen aus spätalttestamentlicher Zeit.* Göttingen: Vandenhoeck & Ruprecht, 1994.

Mays, James Luther. *Psalms.* Interpretation 15. Louisville: John Knox, 1994.

McCann, J. Clinton. "The Book of Psalms: Introduction, Commentary, and Reflections." Pages 639–1280 in *1 & 2 Maccabees; Introduction to Hebrew Poetry; Job; Psalms.* Vol. 4 of *NIB.* Nashville: Abingdon Press, 1996.

———. "Books I–III and the Editorial Purpose of the Hebrew Psalter." Pages 93–107 in *The Shape and Shaping of the Psalter.* Edited by J. Clinton McCann. JSOTSup 159. Sheffield: Sheffield Academic Press, 1993.

Meynet, Roland. *Rhetorical Analysis: An Introduction to Biblical Rhetoric.* JSOTSup 256. Sheffield: Sheffield Academic Press, 1998.

Miller, Patrick D. "The End of the Psalter: A Response to Erich Zenger." *JSOT* 80 (1998) 103–110

———. . "Synonymous-Sequential Parallelism in the Psalms." *Bib* 61 (1980) 256–60.

Muilenburg, James. "Form Criticism and Beyond." *JBL* 88 (1969) 1–18. Repr. Pages 27–44 in *Hearing and Speaking the Word: Selections from the Works of James Muilenburg.* Edited by Thomas F. Best. Chico: CA: Scholars, 1984.

O'Connor, Michael. *Hebrew Verse Structure.* Winona Lake, IN: Eisenbrauns, 1980.

Osgood, Howard. "Dashing the Little Ones Against the Rock." *Princeton Theological Review* 1 (1903) 23–37.

Raabe, Paul R. *Psalms Structures: A Study of Psalms with Refrains.* JSOTSup 104. Sheffield: JSOT Press, 1990.

Renfroe, Fred. "Persiflage in Psalm 137." Pages 509–27 in *Ascribe to the Lord: Biblical and Other Studies in Memory of Peter C. Craigie.* Edited by Lyle Eslinger and J. Glen Taylor. JSOTSup 67. Sheffield: JSOT Press, 1988.

Rensburg, J. F. J. van. "History as Poetry: A Study of Psalm 136." Pages 80–90 in *Exodus 1–15: Text and Context.* Edited by J. J. Burden. Pretoria: Old Testament Society of South Africa, 1987.

Risse, Siegfried. "'Wohl dem, der deine kleinen Kinder packt und sie am Felsen zerschmettert': zur Auslegungsgeschichte von Ps 137:9." *BibInt* 14 (2006) 364–84.

Sabourin, Leopold. *The Psalms: Their Origin and Meaning.* Vol. 2. Staten Island, NY: Alba House, 1969.

Savran, George. "'How Can We Sing a Song of the Lord?': The Strategy of Lament in Psalm 137." *ZAW* 112 (2000) 43–58.

Scoralick, Ruth. "Hallelujah für einen gewalttätigen Gott? zur Theologie von Psalm 135 und 136." *BZ* 46 (2002) 253–72.

Segert, Stanislav. "Poetry and Arithmetic: Psalms 29 and 137." Pages 165–81 in *Mythos im Alten Testament.* Edited by Armin Lange, Hermann Lichtenberger, and Diethard Römheld. Berlin: de Gruyter, 1999.

Bibliography

Seybold, Klaus. *Die Wallfahrtpsalmen: Studien zur Enstehungsgeschichte von Psalm 120-134*. Biblische-Theologische Studien 3. Neukirchen-Vluyn: Neukirchener Verlag, 1978.

Shea, William H. "Qinah Meter and Strophic Structure in Psalm 137." *HAR* 8 (1984) 199–214.

Snearly, Michael K. *The Return of the King: Messianic Expectation in Book V of the Psalter*. LHBOTS 624. London: Bloomsbury T & T Clark, 2015.

Steenkamp, Y. "Violence and Hatred in Psalm 137: The Psalm in its Ancient Social Context." *Verbum et Ecclesia* 25 (2004) 294–310.

Terrien, Samuel. *The Psalms: Strophic Structure and Theological Commentary*. Eerdmans Critical Commentary. Grand Rapids, MI: Eerdmans, 2003.

Trible, Phyllis. *Rhetorical Criticism: Context, Method, and the Book of Jonah*. Minneapolis: Fortress, 1994.

Waltke, Bruce K. and M. O'Connor. *An Introduction to Biblical Hebrew Syntax*. Winona Lake, IN: Eisenbrauns, 1990.

Watson, Wilfred G. E. *Classical Hebrew Poetry: A Guide to Its Techniques*. JSOTSup 26. Sheffield: JSOT Press, 1984. Reprint, London: T & T Clark, 2005.

Weiser, Artur. *The Psalms: A Commentary*. Translated by Herbert Hartwell. OTL. Philadelphia: Westminster Press; London: SCM Press, 1962.

Wilson, Gerald H. *The Editing of the Hebrew Psalter*. Chico, CA: Scholars, 1985.

———. "Shaping the Psalter: A Consideration of Editorial Linkage in the Books of Psalms." Pages 72–82 in *The Shape and Shaping of the Psalter*. Edited by J. Clinton McCann. JSOTSup 159. Sheffield: JSOT Press, 1993.

Zenger, Erich. "The Composition and Theology of the Fifth Book of Psalms, Psalms 107-145." *JSOT* 80 (1998) 77–102.

Zimmerli, Walther. "Zwillingspsalmen." Pages 105–13 in *Wort, Lied, und Gottesspruch: Beiträge zu Psalmen und Propheten*. Edited by Josef Schreiner. Wurzburg / Stuttgart: Echter, 1972.

www.ingramcontent.com/pod-product-compliance
Lightning Source LLC
Chambersburg PA
CBHW072149160426
43197CB00012B/2312